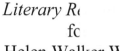
fc
Helen Walker Webb

MW00647706

Second Springs Arts Festival, 2016
Gold Award for Narrative
> "The Porch"

Piedmont Plus Senior Games and Silver Arts, 2017
Gold for Favorite Memory
> "Ziplining"
Silver for Essay
> "What Are You Doing"

Dixie Classic Fair, 2017
Red Ribbon
> "Traits Learned from My Parents"

Piedmont Plus Senior Games and Silver Arts, 2018
Gold for Essay
> "The Book"

Silver for Short Story
> "The NSDBC"

Bronze for Favorite Memory
> "The Pocketbook"

Piedmont Plus Senior Games and Silver Arts, 2019
Gold for Essay
> "Buying a New Car"

Gold for Life Experience
        "The Big Stick"

Piedmont Plus Senior Games and Silver Arts, 2020
Gold for Essay
        "The Lifeboat"

Bronze for Life Experience
        "Memories of Beloved Companion"

Piedmont Plus Senior Games and Silver Arts, 2021
Gold for Essay
        "The Pumpkin"

Piedmont Plus Senior Games and Silver Arts, 2022
Bronze for Life Experience
        "Birthday Experience"

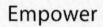

Empower

Publishing

Enjoy
Helen Walker Webb

Also from Helen Walker Webb

Old Ladies Can Zipline Too

and *Empower Publishing*

From Birdwatcher to Jailbird

By

Helen Walker Webb

Empower Publishing
Winston-Salem

Empower

Publishing

Empower Publishing
302 Ricks Drive
Winston-Salem, NC 27103

First Empower Publishing Books edition published
September, 2022
Empower Publishing, Feather Pen, and all production design are trademarks.

For information regarding bulk purchases of this book, digital purchase and special discounts, please contact the publisher at publish.empower.now@gmail.com

Cover design by Pan Morelli

Manufactured in the United States of America
ISBN 978-1-63066-544-9

This book is dedicated to Tim and Lisa, my children, who have encouraged and supported me in my writing.

—Helen Walker Webb

Table of Contents

Foreword

These essays are glimpses of my life as I've moved from watching "my birds" to making the decision to sell my house of 55 years and move to the Happy Home Retirement Community. Within four months of that move, COVID struck and the "great lockdown" began. Living through these past three years has been like riding a roller coaster: emotions swirling up and down, around and around, stopping only to take on more passengers. Come, fasten your seat belt and ride with me as I tell you how it has been.

My Birds

I love my birds and they love me. I know they do. When the two birdfeeders are nearly empty and I go out into the yard, one bird will start singing "Here she comes." Then others sing the same song from tree to tree, bush to bush, wire to wire, even to the trees in neighboring yards. "She is coming, she is coming." The closer I get to the building in which I keep the seed, the louder the chorus. As soon as the feeders are filled and back in place, birds begin to appear almost out of nowhere. It doesn't matter if I stay out in the yard or not; the birds feel confident and safe to come to the feeders. If a predator appears, they all rush off in a flutter and watch from a safe place.

The sunroom is my favorite place to be in the house. Here I read, watch TV, eat lunch and supper, talk on the phone and watch my birds. The birds have their own way of communicating with each other. Some birds seem to come in twos or threes, others come alone. Male cardinals seem to rule the roost. One will swoop down on birds feeding, flutter his wings and chase the others off. Sometimes he calls to his mate to come join him. The ones he chased off don't go far but sit on the cable wire or the rooftop. They wait till the cardinal flies off and then return to the feeder. Some of the bigger birds appear to wait in the tall trees and then swoop down, grab a seed and fly off to return later. The smaller birds sit on the wire and await their turn. The yellow birds usually come in pairs. Sometimes as many as four birds will be feeding at the same feeder. They are little and do not need a perch. They can attach themselves to anyplace on the feeder. The smaller birds often wait in the holly bushes as opposed to the larger birds that wait in the trees or on wires.

Many birds come to the feeders at regular times of the day. They seem to have a mid-morning second breakfast, late lunch and early supper. In between, they snack. Sometimes a family of birds will come. The parents will swoop in, clear out any other birds and then the young ones will appear. I have noticed one small brown bird that comes alone when no other birds appear to be close by. I've named her "the biblical bird at the well." She seems to come from nowhere and flies to nowhere. There's a cardinal that will come and, when he leaves, he flies to a tall rhododendron, then to several low tree branches, and then to high tall tree limbs. Eventually he comes back on the same path. Bird watching has brought me hours of enjoyment. I do wonder if the birds call me "Miss Helen" or "The Seed Lady."

Buying a New Car

In late July 2018, the air conditioning quit in my 2003 Mercury Sable. I was told the car needed about $2,000 of repair work. My plan was to wait until September 18, 2018 and then buy a new car. September 18 was the last day of a three-year insurance penalty for a prior mishap. For several weeks I was able to park in the shade and to do my errands in the mornings. Then the August heat arrived and waiting became more uncomfortable.

In the meantime, I had talked with several people about what kind of car to buy. Honda Accord was the unanimous winner. Several neighbors offered to go car shopping with me as did Lisa, my daughter. Eighty-two-year-old women should not go car shopping alone. I made an appointment with a highly recommended Honda salesman but was late arriving as I had driven past the dealership and gotten lost trying to find my way back without having to make a dreaded left-hand turn.

The salesman warmly greeted Lisa and me. He asked what kind of car I wanted: the size, the motor, the various accessories, the color, etc. All of which are important to most people but not me. I told him, "I want a dependable car that will start on the first try and one I can find in a parking lot." Actually, I didn't want a yellow, white or black car. Soon he had a car for me to test drive. Because I didn't have a color preference, he chose a car the color he liked: champagne. Lisa liked the color. We were making progress.

The salesman drove the car out the back parking lot on to Old Salisbury Road to another parking lot where we switched drivers and I drove several miles and then back to the second parking lot. Before the test drive, the salesman showed me some of the features and how to start and stop the car. I was not able to start and stop the car as smoothly as he was. Several times he turned a little pale and his hands grabbed the back of the seat.

Pricing and paperwork took forever. Lisa was constantly texting or googling on her phone. I was concerned that the insurance coverage be correct. The insurance agent wanted information I didn't know so Lisa dealt with him. Unbeknown to me, Lisa's husband called and talked to the dealership manager twice to make sure we were being taken care of. Eventually a nice man came to show us how the car worked. Lisa told him, as well as the salesman, to show me only what I needed to know and not any bells or whistles. I vetoed installing my cell phone number. I certainly did not want a phone ringing when I'm driving. The nice man adjusted the lights to automatic, the air to automatic, the windshield wipers, and the radio to play only the two stations to which I listen. He showed us how to lock and unlock the car, trunk, gas tank and how to work the windows. It all went in one ear and out the other. It was just too overwhelming.

After the demonstration, there was more paperwork to complete, most of which involved the business manager going over all the details and asking about add-ons. Lisa told me to say no to every add-on, which I did. Feeling everything was under control, Lisa left. It took another hour to sign everything and wait for the car to be cleaned and ready for delivery.

About 3:00 p.m., the nice man drove the car and me to the end of the back parking lot. (Another employee followed us to take the nice man back to the dealership.) The salesman had not wanted me to leave by way of Peters Creek Parkway. I guess he was afraid I would wreck in front of the dealership. I did know my way home and arrived safely. I went in the house, got the key to the safety deposit box, drove to the bank, parked the car, got the old car title from my safety deposit box, got in the car and the car wouldn't start. After several choice words, it started. I drove directly to Harris Teeter, as Thursday is grocery day, and got my groceries. I was able to unlock the trunk and the car. This time the car started.

During the first three months of owning this car, I lost it in the parking lot only once. I did not try to turn on the radio as I wasn't sure which button to push. After many mistakes, I learned how to work the windshield wipers as well as how to unlock the doors from the inside. The first time I got gas, I could not remember which picture to push to get the gas tank door unlocked and had to get the manual out of the glove box. It took ten minutes to find the answer. Fortunately, no one was in line behind me. The second time I got gas, I forgot how the gas tank door opened after the picture was pushed and asked a man at the pump ahead of me if he could help me. The next time after I got gas, I couldn't make the gas tank door stay closed. The car continued to yell at me and to distract me by flashing pictures on the dashboard. Sometimes I could figure out why and sometimes I could not.

After eight-and-a-half months of a rather rocky relationship, the new car and I have become more comfortable with each other. The windshield wipers and I are now very good friends. The headlights are making progress in establishing rapport with me. Somehow I had gotten the automatic function for the head lights off track and they were on all the time. A friend showed me what was wrong and I am now driving with them on automatic. One rainy late afternoon I could not tell if the lights were on or off. I got out of the car and looked. They were on. I now know where the little blue light is on the dashboard that lights up if the lights are on.

Not only are the lights and wipers now my friends, I can also turn on the radio. Just am not sure how to change stations. To top it off, the fourth time I got gas, I did it all by myself: unlocked the gas-tank door, opened the gas tank door and locked the gas tank door. I was so proud of myself! The next day when I got in the car to go to the grocery store, it would not start. I pushed the button for the red light; I pushed on the brake, back and forth. Sometime the dashboard would light up with messages and I tried to do what it said and nothing would work. Finally I called a neighbor who came over and the car started right away for him. He suggested that I move the seat closer to the front, which I did and now the car usually starts on the first try.

Because the seat has been moved, the side view mirrors need adjustment. That remains a feat in progress.

One rainy Thursday, I pulled up to the side of Harris Teeter to have my groceries put in the trunk. I was able to find the button to unlock the truck from inside the car. I watched in the rearview mirror as the clerk put the groceries in and shut the lid but I did not see him put in the crate of tangerines. I pulled up out of the way, got out of the car to unlock the trunk, but could not get the trunk open from the outside. I gave up and drove home. The trunk opened fine and contained all the groceries.

Cars changed tremendously between 2003 and 2018 as did technology. The transition to a new car has been a struggle but I've come a long way with learning how to drive this car. Tomorrow I plan to make an appointment with the nice man to show me how to change radio stations and what all of those pictures on the dashboard mean.

The Book Signing Party

Self-publishing my first book, a collection of short essays and narratives, has been a fun-filled adventure full of new experiences. A highlight of this adventure was the book signing party that Barbara, my Friday bridge partner, and Sue, my bridge mentor for two years, hosted for me on a Wednesday morning in September.

The party was at Barbara's home from 10:00 a.m. until noon. Most of those invited were church friends or women who play duplicate bridge with me at the recreation centers. This time frame made it convenient for the Wednesday bridge players to come, buy a book, eat a snack and then go play bridge. Barbara's house has an open floor plan with large windows which is perfect for such a gathering. Particularly impressive were the two tall vases of graceful tropical flowers. One was on the baby grand piano where Copper, the cat, would walk around and around without ever disturbing the flowers. A lovely arrangement of roses was in the center of the dining room table which was laden with a variety of party sandwiches, fruit and pastries. A steady stream of people, men and women, came in and out the entire time.

The Friday before the party, I had taken a new bridge wig to Phyllis, my wig lady, to be styled for the upcoming event. I told Phyllis about the event and invited her to the party. Phyllis has published two books and had given me some tips on how to publicize a book. I gave her Barbara's address which she said she would put in her GPS and have no problem finding the house. We also discussed her autographing the Wig Lady story and how special a book with both her autograph and mine would be.

I was so excited when she arrived about halfway through the party. I stopped signing and announced that the Wig Lady had arrived. She promptly stopped me and said that she was not the Wig Lady. I replied: "Oh, yes you are." Then I told those gathered, if they wanted, I was certain that Phyllis would autograph the Wig Lady story for them and that they would have a very special book. With that, I went back to my chair and signing books.

Later, I noticed the Wig Lady was gone and thought it strange she had stayed such a short time. What I did not know was that, before leaving, she had gone into the kitchen and told Barbara that she did not know what was wrong with Helen. She was not the Wig Lady and had never worn a wig. She was actually a lady who plays bridge on Tuesdays and Fridays. In fact, I had played against her and her partner the day before. Except for their lips, the two ladies look enough alike to be twins.

It was a fun party. I sold 28 of the 29 books I had brought. And yes, some did go from the party straight to the bridge table.

The Lifeboat

The technical definition of a lifeboat is "a boat carried on a ship for use if the ship has to be abandoned." Lifeboats are standard equipment for ships to be used in the event of an emergency. So what do lifeboats do? They keep people afloat until help can rescue them from a situation. Most people will never need a lifeboat to keep them from the depths of the sea.

To my small writing group, the lifeboat has a much broader meaning. Several years ago, someone brought a small, rubber lifeboat to class. It's about seven inches long and four inches wide and fits nicely in one hand. It's soft but firm to the touch. On the side is printed "We Are All in This Lifeboat Together." Each month someone is selected to take the boat home with them until the next meeting. The boat has little meaning just seeing it but the true meaning reveals itself when you are chosen to take it home.

At home, looking at the boat, you see the love of your fellow writers. You see their concern for your problems. You see encouragement. You see care. You see friendship. You can hold the boat and feel its soft but firm body and know that the group has a soft spot in their hearts for you and a firm desire to uphold you.

Lifeboats are for short term use…to save a life in danger. Our lifeboat does not save us from deep waters but from other hazards such as discouragement, frustration, feelings of loss, confusion or of being overwhelmed with life's events. It reminds us that, at times, we all are in need of a lifeboat. I now think of our group as a lifeboat…linking arms, holding tightly, keeping everyone afloat. Our stories are the passengers in this very special boat.

My Pocketbook

Over the years, I have accumulated many pocketbooks of different sizes, shapes, materials and colors. In the olden days, one matched shoes and pocketbooks. Not so now. Currently the same pocketbook can go everywhere, except for Sundays and some even on Sundays. Recently, I've changed my go-everywhere pocketbook because the weight of that pocketbook was heavier than the one I'm now using.

The purpose of a pocketbook is to carry one's necessary items. On bridge days, I include my eight-by-four-inch bridge folder, my envelope with bridge money for the month, a bottle of water and a sweater. These are in addition to the everyday items. A small cloth change purse contains two hearing aid batteries, a card of several Gas-x tablets and several cough drops. This little purse is always placed in a zipper compartment in the pocketbook. Also in that compartment are an emery board and several Band-Aids. A small bottle of hand sanitizer, a rain scarf and a small container of Tylenol are in another compartment. The large zipper compartment holds my wig comb, pen, keys and leather change purse. This change purse has two zipper compartments. One is for loose change and a couple of $1.00 bills. The larger compartment contains my two credit cards, driver's license, car registration card, car insurance card, AAA card, health insurance, dental insurance and Medicare cards. These cards are rubber banded together. A second group of cards, mostly reward cards with a $20 bill folded on top, also held together with a rubber band, fit tightly in the purse.

The key ring holds my house key, storm door key, the car bob and sixteen reward type cards. Depending on the pocketbook, I put the ring in a separate compartment by itself. A small unopened package of facial tissue, several pieces of facial tissue and a handkerchief go wherever there is room. (The packaged tissue is kept in the event I'm in a stall in the ladies' room with no toilet paper. I believe in being prepared.) My pocket calendar and cell phone slip in against one side of the purse. A package of Nabs and crackers always are in a side container as is a small plastic folder of restaurant coupons. Depending on the weather, sunglasses or an umbrella complete the contents of my pocketbook.

If I'm going to the grocery store, a grocery coupon folder goes in the pocketbook. On Sundays, the food, Tylenol and the pocket calendar are replaced with my Sunday School booklet. I don't like large pocketbooks so I must pack carefully.

The Big Stick

I had been in the backyard picking up sticks which had fallen during the cold, wet and windy month of January 2019. It was a nice day to be outside: cold but sunny. The ground was slightly damp but not muddy. The yard waste container was now full of broken down sticks and branches. My plan was to fill the bird feeders and then go inside and study my bridge book. The plan changed when I saw the big stick in the woods at the edge of my property. It was long with several branches at the end.

The city truck which picks up fallen tree limbs hadn't been in the neighborhood in weeks. The leaf truck was scheduled to come the next day. I walked to the stick and considered throwing it over the fence into the adjoining property but I have never approved of throwing things over the fence even though the land is overgrown with all kinds of trees and vines. Deer frequently jump over the fence into my yard. I decided to carry the stick to the curb.

It wasn't a heavy stick but it was about twelve feet long and somewhat gangly. The branches at the top made it difficult to maneuver. About halfway up the back yard, I decided to break it. By breaking it, I could add it to my neighbor's stick pile at the curb. My curb was full of leaves. I put as much of the stick as I could on the ground and my foot on the stick and, with all my strength, bent the stick over to break. It did not break easily. When it suddenly broke, the stick and I went flying in different directions.

It took a little time for me to regain my composure and realize what had happened. As I untangled my legs, a sharp pain shot through my pelvis and right leg. No other body part seemed to be affected. Looking around, I realized I was all alone with no one in sight. I started yelling "Help!" and waving my arms in hopes that someone might hear me. I was the perfect picture of the lady yelling for help in the medical alarm button ads. My only choice was to crawl up to the front yard which I did using my left leg and upper body. Although I was yelling and waving my arms and cars were passing, no one came to help. Because the yard slants downward from the curb and shrubbery is along the side, I was not easy to see. Determined not to freeze, I crawled to the front porch steps and pulled myself up to a prone position against the handrail. Here, I began yelling again. Eventually a neighbor came out of her house and saw me and came over. Sarah called EMS, got my pocketbook and cell phone and then locked the front door.

EMS came and carted me off to the hospital. I stayed six nights and then went to Trinity Elms for two weeks of rehab. The fall had broken a bone in my pelvis. When I came home, I could see the large parts of the broken stick from my sunroom. Every time I saw them, I got mad at myself. When I progressed from the walker to a cane, I went out in the yard and moved the two sticks from the grass to the pine needles at the side of the house. Last week I was able to carry both sticks to the curb where they can just stay and wait for the big truck to carry them out of my sight.

The Straw

About eight years ago, I carefully wrapped a bale of straw with two extra-large white plastic bags and stored it in the crawl space of my house. I planned to use the bale the following Halloween in a front porch decoration. I was going to place a cute fabric straw man on top of the straw and a jack-o-lantern surrounded with fall flowers in front of the straw. That never happened. Now, I needed that straw.

The plumber had just finished installing a new water line from the water meter at the street diagonally across my perfectly groomed front yard to the house. A two foot deep, two foot wide trench had been dug and the line installed, then covered with dirt. Lastly grass seed had been spread. The seed had not been covered with straw. All newly seeded dirt needs straw.

Because the plumbers had to work in the crawl space, I had removed everything out of the crawl space to the utility building. The carefully wrapped straw was in the wheelbarrow in the utility building which was overflowing with stuff. I managed to get the wheelbarrow out and to the front yard, almost scrapping the side of my car. I took one plastic bag off half the bale and with scissors cut the reddish-orange twine. Holding as much straw as I could and beginning at the street, I started spreading straw. I had to take a break every ten minutes to rest my back and cool off. Soon I noticed that the straw was streaked with bright

17

white and silver pieces. I began to think that maybe this wasn't natural straw but decorative Halloween straw. Nevertheless, I finished covering the dirt. Several hours later, the silver and white pieces were still shining and reflecting light. I decided it must be artificial straw and began picking up the straw and putting it into the brown garbage cart.

A neighbor had been watching from afar and, seeing me in the yard, walked over to get the scoop on the situation. After telling him about the water leak, I asked him what he thought of the straw. He thought it was not straw as it certainly was not rotten and old straw would be rotten by now. He offered to rake the remainder the next day for me. Then another neighbor came over and said it was straw but that, if it was as old as I had said, it was too old to use and I should buy another bale and put it on heavier than I had. Moreover, he said I should not put the straw in the brown garbage cart but in the green yard cart. According to him, straw is not garbage but yard waste.

Decisions, decisions. That night I thought that if the straw was artificial, why would it have been wrapped in the reddish-orange twine used for pine needles. Then I thought that brooms are made of orange straw and they last a long time without changing colors. By morning, I decided the straw was not artificial straw but just old straw. Using what I had put in the garbage cart plus some of the additional old straw which was in the bag, once again I put out straw. This time I covered the entire trench with a heavy layer of straw.

Much to my surprise, a week later green grass began to appear. Not able to use a rake, I began picking up straw again. After getting off the heaviest of the straw, I used my hand to rake through the new grass. Ten days have gone by since green grass began to appear. Each day new patches of grass replace brown dirt. Each day, handful by handful, most of the straw has now gone into the yard cart....ten minutes picking up straw, ten minutes resting my back several times a day. Soon the straw will disappear and my yard will return to being the "showcase yard" of the neighborhood.

Downsizing

Downsizing is a new experience for me. I've always "upsized." After college I lived in an apartment furnished with "hand-me-downs" and an inexpensive living room suite. When Tom and I decided to marry, we contracted to have a house built in the newly-opened British Woods development. We moved into the house two days after our marriage and never left. I've been in the house for 55 years. Over the years some furniture has been replaced, a room added and stuff has accumulated to overflowing. We added an out-building which also overflows with stuff: good stuff, might-be-valuable stuff, interesting stuff, important stuff, might-need stuff, great-great-grandfather's stuff. You name it. I've got it right down to all my tax returns back to 1958.

I'm getting old and the time has come to seriously consider a different lifestyle involving living again in an apartment. But, not to fear, I'm making progress in my downsizing. Two weeks ago, I reorganized my four-drawer desk and disposed of enough outdated important papers to fill the blue recycle container half full as well as a bag of very important papers to be shredded. Two of the four drawers contain good stuff which, when the time comes, will probably go to Goodwill...but those drawers are organized. That was a two-day project. My one-day project was reading old greeting cards. I threw out 141 and kept 75. Last Saturday Lisa graciously took her baby book and all the stuff I'd saved with it. It had been under a skirted chair in the playroom. The skirted couch hides silver serving trays and a flat leather zipper bag of unframed prints which came from my mother's apartment 32 years ago. This week I worked on the stuff under my bed. I threw away one of six plastic bags. Now one holds a blanket and another holds a throw. I also moved the three decorative paper birthday bags to the Christmas bags under a different bed. Two folded flat boxes from under the dresser got thrown into the blue recycle bin and a denim jumper went in the Goodwill box. Two rather large hanging mirrors, one 1954 suitcase full of off-season socks, one shoebox full of extra Christmas cards, address lists and return labels, two sewing boxes and a large flat box of gift-wrapping supplies remain under the bed. I can now see under the bed from one side to the other. The bed skirt hides these items.

For several weeks I've been trying to find a new home for my doll collection. A doll museum in Spencer may take them, but I'm not certain the person I spoke with understood the rather large number of dolls involved. I've worked on the dolls, taking them out of the glass bookcase, looking them over and seeing what I actually had. There must be a 100 dolls needing adoption. Yesterday Lisa took two dolls and a trophy from high school which she thinks is hers. Today Tim took the Carlos Lee bobblehead doll, one of twelve Warthog-related bobblehead dolls Tom had acquired. They live on the top of the doll case still in their original boxes. Tim also took the two fastest matchbox cars and several small plastic army men. These toys were stored with their friends in a cabinet in the playroom.

Downsizing is somewhat of an ugly word. Although I'm making progress, I feel like it is going to be a daunting journey but, hopefully, with a happy ending.

The Skirt

It was Sunday morning. I was looking forward to a peaceful morning at Sunday School, church services and then lunch. The prior several weeks had completely exhausted me. I had been busy getting my house ready to sell and trying to sell my baby-grand piano. The "For Sale" sign had gone up on Monday and I had two showings earlier in the week.

I had planned what I was going to wear Saturday night after I had read the Sunday School lesson. I knew which pocketbook, shoes, skirt, blouse and scarf I would wear. I had forgotten what jewelry to wear and where I had packed my good jewelry. My timing was thrown off at 8:15 a.m. when an agent called to say that she wanted to show the house between 1:00 and 2:00 p.m. What should have been a smooth morning became hurried.

My figured purple skirt always hangs on the same covered coat hanger with the three-shaded purple wraparound scarf, and a matching purple pullover long sleeve knit top. Next to that hanger is a cream-colored short sleeve blouse. Although the skirt is of a lightweight material, it can be worn year-round except for winter. In hot weather, I wear the short sleeve blouse and carry the scarf to use when in air conditioning.

When I opened the closet door, the purple skirt was not with the purple top. The scarf was there and the cream blouse was there but no purple skirt. In its place was my black and cream skirt. I looked the entire length of the closet and the closet floor thinking the skirt may have fallen off the hanger. No skirt. I went to another closet and looked very carefully; one coat hanger at a time. No purple skirt. I went back to the first closet and looked again, coat hanger by coat hanger. It was not with the winter clothes, nor with the summer clothes. The skirt was not to be found. Time was running out. There was nothing to do but to wear the black and cream skirt with the cream top and purple scarf. The colors and pattern of this skirt are not a favorite of mine but I do wear it occasionally. I finished dressing except for the skirt and jewelry, which I couldn't find. I took the black and cream skirt off the hanger and laid it on the bed. The skirt has an elastic waist. As I put my hands between the front and back of the skirt, I realized it was made of two layers. There was my purple skirt! The skirt is reversible. Sometimes we get so involved with a multitude of things; we don't see what is right in front of us.

PS: I was 2.5 minutes late for Sunday School.

Halloween 2019

For many years, I had been called "Witchey-pooh" by the neighborhood children. I enjoyed dressing up as a witch and handing out treats at Halloween. Halloween 2019 was different as I took a memorable flight on my broomstick to Happy Home Lane. The ride of about ten minutes was the beginning of a new adventure…living in a retirement community.

This adventure has necessitated learning many new things, first of which was how to find my apartment from the main entrance. The building is L-shaped, so there are several halls and an elevator which must be navigated. The elevator doors are extra slow to close unless one knows to push the DOOR CLOSE button before pushing the floor number. Next, after nearly choking myself trying to lock the apartment door with the key on the lanyard around my neck, a neighbor showed me how to push a button on the inside of the door handle before shutting the door. Keeping up with the keys is a real trick. I am not going to wear them around my neck like an old lady with half a brain! I've learned to work the dryer, microwave, stovetop burners but not the oven. Nor do I know how to work the disposal. It has been 45 years since I used one. My daughter showed me how to regulate the heat. I had not looked in the correct place. The storage room for extra or not often used items is close by but one must get the key at the concierge desk. The door to the garbage chute is around the corner and several doors down the hall. Garbage must be doubled bagged and tied before being sent down the chute. The blue recycle bins are in the janitor room at the far end of the hall. Fire escape stairwells are at either end of the hall. Ground level exits are one floor down. One is fairly close to my apartment.

I quickly learned to find the dining room and just as quickly learned to plan to spend an hour or more for supper. People seem to enjoy socializing. I've learned my new address and how to use the flicker to get the gate to the development open. That was a real challenge. I've not learned any car parking skills. For 55 years I parked my car in a driveway. Soon I should be able to learn where all my belongings are located. Learning parking skills is questionable.

The Rollator

Recently I've become fascinated with rollators. A rollator is a "top of the line" walker. It is made of metal as opposed to aluminum. It has front and back wheels, hand operated brakes and a padded seat. The padded seat on the smaller model is about 11 by 11 inches and on the larger one, 13 x 11 inches. It can be folded if necessary. Rollators come in at least two sizes and the height can be adjusted. The front bar is curved outward. Because they have front and back wheels, they roll smoothly.

Until I moved to a retirement community, I thought my pocketbook could hold all that a person could possibly need. I was wrong. The residents who use rollators really can carry everything they might need for an entire day or longer. The larger seat folds upward and under it is a metal basket which can be removed. The basket is a little smaller than the seat. Most owners place a heavy cardboard box (a large shoe box does nicely) in the metal basket. Depending on the person and their activities, a multitude of items can be placed in the box such as, a day's worth of medication (prescription and non-prescription), small boxes of cereal, a bagel or two, a banana or other fresh fruit, a cup of yogurt and I suspect some other personal items. (I've never actually looked inside one.) Some people place hot coffee on top of the seat. They are the ones going straight back to their apartments or to the library to sit and read the newspaper.

In addition to the seat box, there might be a narrow metal basket on the front between the handlebars. In this, a person could place reading material such as the daily newspaper, mail, the calendar of events for the month, the weekly menu, as well as writing materials. Hanging in front of this basket and on the sides of the rollator are canvas bags. Although decorative, the bags are still very useful. They are used to carry such things as a wallet, cell phone, hearing aid batteries, pens, pencils, scissors, screwdriver, pliers, cosmetics and who knows what else. Some are decorated with a variety of objects, even a stuffed animal peeping out of the bag. I think the decorations are used to identify the rollators when parked with several others.

Rollators and similar types of walkers are very useful. They allow a person who otherwise would be confined to their room to be out and about, living a full independent life. People using oxygen can place their oxygen supply in the basket. Because the seat can be used on which to place packages, a person can shop as well as sit if they get tired. I've seen a few people sitting when they were waiting in line to be seated for dinner. Recently a lady came to play bridge and brought her shuffling machine in her rollator basket. Shuffling a deck of card is hard on stiff hands. She parked her rollator along the wall and walked the few steps to the bridge table. Many people can walk a few steps on their own but not very far. Others are not steady walking and need the rollator for support. Rollators were a wonderful invention.

My First Happy Home Adventure

My first adventure on the Happy Home Retirement Community bus was a trip to the Southern Supreme Fruitcake Factory. The trip was advertised as a tour of the factory, sampling of the food and shopping, all occurring after lunch at Elois. I had a feeling that lunch at Elois was going to be a big deal and it was. Elois is about a twenty-minute drive from the Fruitcake Factory which is in Bear Creek. Exactly where is Elois? I know only that it is just about one and a half hours down Highway 421 from Winston-Salem.

Elois is a local truck stop well known for its good food, cheap prices and quick service. Church buses, community activity buses and cars share the large parking lot with all kinds and sizes of trucks. There is absolutely nothing nearby but the road. Looks like a truck stop: is a truck stop.

As soon as we entered, the staff began putting tables together and moving chairs to seat our party of thirteen. We could hardly get in our chairs before the waitresses were taking drink orders and handing out menus. Between pouring water and tea, they were taking orders. People had to decide quickly what to order. As we waited for our food, I noticed that placed strategically behind the counters were large containers of water and tea that the waitresses could pour into their pitchers without having to go to a central location. The middle-aged waitresses just seemed to fly from one group of customers to another. People were constantly coming and going. Our orders were served quickly. I had ordered a small (4 ounce) cheeseburger with slaw, chilly and mustard. It was hot and delicious and cost less than $4.00.

As we were gathering to leave, I noticed a man looking at the group and shaking his head. I caught his eye and said," It's a motley group, isn't it?" He just kept on shaking his head.

The Happy Home bus seats twelve people and the driver. Of the twelve, one was riding an electric three-wheel scooter, four were using walkers, and three were using canes. We all had to be careful walking on the uneven parking lot. It was a happy but motley crew.

Between Elois and the fruitcake factory, we saw lots of cows but no bears. Once at the factory, most gathered for the tour but a few went straight to the large shopping area. The tour guide explained that her mother had been a beautician and had given her clients homemade fruitcake. The clients liked the fruitcakes so much that her mother started a small fruitcake business which grew into the now large well known Southern Supreme Fruit Cake Factory. The story was similar in many ways to Mrs. Hanes' Moravian Cookie Factory. The tour was interesting. They use 200 eggs a day in the batter for the fruit cake. The fruitcake is mostly nuts and very little, if any, fruit. The company has expanded its products into nuts, jellies, candies and cheese straws.

At the end of the tour, we were directed to the sample room where we were given a two-bite piece of fruitcake with a small cheese straw on top and a small cup of either coffee or hot apple cider. I loved the apple cider. Then we were directed to the sales room. No food was allowed in the sales room. Hence, I found a chair and finished my apple cider before venturing into the elaborate showroom.

The large area was commercialized to the limits: all kinds of goodies in all size packages. Fruitcake did not seem to be the main item. The aisles were crowded with walkers and people buying tons of goodies. I was a little envious of the folks with walkers as they were able to put all their purchases on the walker's seat and hang their pocketbooks over the handles. I had to tug and juggle mine. Getting back on the bus with our bags of goodies was not easy but with the help of others, everyone managed to get to their seats. The trip home was uneventful. Lunch at Elois was the highlight of the trip for me. It fascinated me as to how efficient the truck stop operated as well as the different types of people who went in and out of the restaurant. I'm still wondering, if all things are considered, whether Mrs. Hanes' Moravian Cookie Factory or Supreme Fruitcake Factory make the most profit.

The Bed

Ten years ago, my husband decided that he needed a Sleep Number Bed. As a result of breaks in his ribs, he needed to sleep with his upper body elevated. An extra-long twin Sleep Number base with mattress was ordered and delivered for his bed. It was the perfect answer for his back. The bed came with two remotes. One regulated the firmness of the mattress and the other raised and lowered the head and foot of the bed. When Tom could no longer go up and down stairs, the bed was moved down to the main living area and, after his death, it was moved to the extra room on the lowest level. Each time the bed was moved, it was necessary to have a specialist come from High Point to move it. The bed was never slept in after Tom's death.

For many years Tom and I had slept in matching extra-long twin beds. When I moved to the Happy Home Community, I decided to use the twin beds in the larger of two bedrooms. That way, there would be beds for visitors if necessary. I had matching quilted bedspreads and dust ruffles for the beds. Tom's bed was a little lower than mine but not enough to concern me. The day of the move, I was told that one of the movers was familiar with Sleep Number beds and would be able to move and set up the bed without having to hire a specialist but a problem developed. Due to non-use and age, the batteries in the two remotes had corroded very badly. With a good cleaning and new batteries, the remote which controlled the air worked but the one which controlled the height adjustments did not. I would have to order a new remote. I wasn't planning on using the bed and it looked good in the room. Adding a new remote went to the bottom of my to-do list.

To raise the height of the Sleep Number bed I carefully folded and placed extra blankets, one of which was a puffy feather quilt, on top of the mattress and covered them with the quilted bedspread. Several weeks later I put some clothes on the side of the bed. Soon I noticed that the bed began to look like it had sunk in a bit. It had. Now I had a real problem, particularly when Conner, my thirteen-year-old grandson decided to lie in the middle and the bed really sank in. Conner looked like he was in a coffin.

I had a decision to make: get the bed repaired or buy a new regular mattress and springs. I had saved and brought the original bed slates with me. After several phone calls, visits to mattress stores and comparisons of costs, I decided to have the bed repaired and ordered the parts. The parts came; the bed workmen came; the new parts were installed and the bed had air. Yeah! I could regulate the firmness but the head would not go up. It was the remote. Too much corrosion had gotten in the second remote. After working with the remote and something under the bed and talking with supervisors on the phone, the men gave up. They said customer service would call me in thirty minutes. Customer service did call and told me there was a new remote which would work with my bed so I ordered it.

Two weeks later, the remote had not arrived. On New Year's Eve, I moved the old remote to a different place on the bedside table and, all of a sudden, the head of the bed began to move. Slowly, slowly it moved almost upright, just like a ghost moving out of the grave. Not knowing why or how, I quickly pushed the down button on the remote. Luckily the head moved down until level with the rest of the bed. The new remote has not arrived.

February Trips

February 18, 2020, was Andy Griffith Day at the Happy Home Retirement Community. The day started at 9:30 a.m. when the Happy Home bus pulled away from the Club House. (We would have left earlier except for the one person who believes in arriving on the exact departing time.) Eleven residents, the activities director and the bus driver filled the bus to capacity. The trip to and from Mt. Airy was uneventful.

We were met at the Andy Griffith Museum by Abigail, our tour guide for the day. A rather small old house on the hillside next to the Andy Griffith Playhouse has been converted into the Andy Griffith Museum. Outside the museum is a beautiful bronze statue of Andy and Opie. The approach to the building is not particularly "old folks friendly" as the walkway from the parking area to the building is rather far and has some curves and cement steps. Eventually we all arrived at the entrance and a bench on which we could rest. The museum is small but contains a multitude of pictures and memorabilia from Andy's life, the Andy Griffith show and other shows in which Andy had appeared. Abigail knew the history and significance of everything in the museum as well as Andy's life. She was excellent!

Interesting to me was the fact that Andy's big start in the theater world was "What It Was Was Football." When I was in college at St. Mary's in Raleigh, NC,

Andy performed "What It Was Was Football" at an assembly program. I loved it then and still do.

The highlight of the trip was having lunch with Betty Lynn who played Thelma Lou. Betty is now 93 and lives at the retirement community where we had lunch. I sat with four others at her table. She was easy to talk with. She told us of many things about the TV program. She had not been under contract with the show. She was paid for only those shows she was in. What she enjoyed most about being in the show was the excellent writers. The actors had three days to learn their lines. Neither backstage prompters nor ad-libbing were allowed. By the third day everyone knew their lines. When Opie first appeared on the show, he was only four and did not read. His parents who were actors taught him his lines and what expressions to use. They were always with him on the set. He was known as an outstanding child actor. After lunch, Betty Lynn had an open question-and-answer session. We were home shortly after 3:30 pm.

Back at Happy Home, Andy Griffith Day continued with a jail set up outside the dining room and pictures around and about. The supper menu featured fried chicken and collard greens, fried pork chop sandwiches and fried whiting with turnip greens, pinto beans and corn bread. Banana pudding was the dessert. To top the day off the Back Porch Bluegrass Band played during supper with some folks dancing and lots of clapping.

Nine days later I was on the Happy Home bus headed to the Himalayan Hideaway located in Winston-Salem. This time we had residents on an electric scooter, a rollator and a cane. All of which was manageable. The cave is located in a small store which has three small rooms: the entrance room, the cave and the tearoom. The cave is designed to make you feel as though you have just landed in a courtyard in Nepal. The eleven of us had to stand close together to fit in the entrance room. Because the floor of the cave is covered with 8,000 pounds of pink salt, before entering the cave we had to either take off our shoes or cover our shoes with shoe covers. Picture please this group of old people, most of whom have trouble bending over, trying to put shoe covers on their shoes while standing. It was lean on me and I'll lean on you. Once we got in the cave and managed not to trip in the salt which acted like sand, we sat in gravity-free lounge chairs looking up at the twinkling starlight as the lights were dimmed and soft music was played. After relaxing and breathing in the salt air for 45 minutes, the lights came on and we were escorted to the tearoom for a cup of hot Asian tea. Several folks had to be helped out of their chairs. It took three people to get one lady up. In the tea room, for those folks who had actually taken their shoes off, there were warm lighted domes on which to rest their feet. Because no one drank the tea, we soon left for the return trip home.

The Andy Griffith trip was fun. The Himalayan Hideaway experience was informative.

Porch Sitting

Here I sit on the front porch of the Club House of the Happy Home Retirement Community. Two flags on high poles on either side of the portico are flapping in the breeze. Trees with their new spring leaves are bending and swaying as the breeze strengthens to a wind. The bright sunshine of this morning has been replaced with clouds covering almost all of the sky. A storm is on the way, a storm of nature and a storm of the COVID-19 virus.

This morning the seven white rocking chairs were filled with a variety of older men, most of who sit on the porch late morning until lunch time and again mid-afternoon to supper time. One side of the porch has three chairs and the other side has four. Small round tables separate the chairs. A wide walkway ending in double doors to the clubhouse separates the two sides. People come and go all the time.

When I arrive, only four people are on the porch. One man, a regular porch-sitter, is sitting alone on the three-chair side. A married couple is sitting on the other side next to a regular lady chair-sitter who has a touch of dementia. The man sitting alone has his legs stretched out with his feet resting on top of the seat of his walker. I sit next to the lady with memory problems. After moving my chair to get more space between us, I begin to write.

39

The lady with the memory problems talks with the other lady. I enjoy sitting and watching the trees and listening for birds to chirp. Only occasionally does a bird chirp which is answered by a chorus of chirping and then silence. The birds must be hunkering down for a big storm. A ninety-year-old lady, a regular chair-sitter who uses a walker, comes and sits on the three-chair side. Then the lady on my right leaves and a regular porch-sitter comes and takes her place.

The breeze begins to blow a few drops of rain. I can feel them. The sidewalk is turning wet. The activity director comes out and I can hear something about wiping chairs and the virus spreading twelve feet instead of six feet. Then she goes inside. I decide to leave before the rain gets worse. By the time I walk the hallway, get the elevator and arrive at my apartment, the sky is getting light. Within an hour, the sun is out and the sky is completely blue. I wish the COVID-19 storm would do the same.

Porches

Porches have always been a part of my life. The word porch brings warm thoughts and feelings to my mind and body. The first house I ever lived in was in Fairmont, West Virginia. I remember seeing pictures of my older brother Billy and his friend sitting on the porch steps holding their hands around their cheeks. They were probably about four years old. Billy and his friends often played on the steps while I was in the playpen. One day while the three of us were on the porch, a neighbor saw a snake at the foot of the steps.

My father died three weeks before my fourth birthday. Mother, Billy, my baby brother Walter and I moved to Charleston, West Virginia to live with my mother's parents. Grandmother and Granddaddy Wood had a large house with a porch across the front of the house, around the corner and down part of the side of the house. The porch had two doors. Both opened into a large entrance room. The side porch is where the family would gather on warm nights after supper. From the porch, you could see Virginia Street and the houses across the street.

Sitting on the porch, sometimes you could hear neighbors talking across the street. The lots on either side of the house were vacant. Most all the families close by knew each other, their children and grandchildren. Sometimes folks would walk up or down the street and stop to chat. Porches were the gathering places.

After World War II ended, mother was able to buy a house one street over and a half a block from Granddaddy's house. This house was much smaller than Granddaddy's and had no side yards. It had a front porch and a screened back porch. On very hot nights I often slept on the back porch. The front porch was wide enough for a glider at one end, a rocking chair and several other porch chairs. Some of the neighbors were long-time friends; some not. There was always something or someone to watch from the porch. (The mail man came twice a day as did the paper boy.) We often visited with neighbors on their porches. Some folks had hanging porch swings. We did not. Air conditioning was a thing of the future. Porches were cool, comfortable and inviting.

My father's family lived in Lynchburg, Virginia. Summers in Lynchburg were much hotter than in Charleston. After supper the children went outside to play until bedtime and the adults sat on the front porch. Often Aunt Alma and Grandmother Walker would sit on the porch and "snap" beans. Uncle Joe had a big vegetable garden with lots of corn, tomatoes and beans. What vegetables the family didn't need were sold at a nearby grocery store. If there was "happy hour," it was on the porch. Just as in Charleston, the front porch was the place to be on a hot summer evening. Supper was never served on the front porch.

After Granddaddy died, Aunt Helen and Uncle Perry's home became the favorite family gathering place. They did not have a front porch but had a large cement back porch closed in with wrought iron railing. It was made on top of the attached one-car garage. Later a roof was added and the porch was glassed in. "Happy Hour" was usually on the porch as was supper. Before it was glassed in, Uncle Perry would grill hamburgers on the porch and Aunt Helen had some cookware she used for porch cooking. Because the porch became such a popular eating place, Uncle Perry cut a rectangular hole in the wall between the kitchen and porch large enough to pass food through. That pass-through saved many steps and time. Eventually Aunt Helen and Uncle Perry would eat breakfast on the porch.

The porch was a fun place to be. The house was located on the top of a hill overlooking the Kanawha River valley and the hills across the river. Uncle Perry would tell us what was going on in the other parts of the city. He could spot police cars, traffic jams, funeral processionals going to the cemetery, football traffic or most anything going on in town. From the porch we could watch trains, planes and boats. Uncle Perry usually could tell us where the trains and boats were going as well as who owned the boats. The porch held lots of laughter and lots of family stories. From the time my children were of kindergarten age, they liked going to Aunt Helen and Uncle Perry's as they could play around and listen to all the chatter, particularly during "happy hour." There was no "happy hour" when visiting my husband's family.

43

After college graduation, I moved to Winston-Salem and rented a second-floor apartment in a four-apartment building. Both second-floor apartments had separate front porches and small back porches. My front porch had attached flower boxes on two sides. I had brought several porch chairs and tables from Charleston. I never planted flowers in the boxes, but I did enjoy sitting on the porch and watching the cars go by. Sometimes I had company to sit on the porch with me.

My husband's family lived on Main Street in Galax, Virginia. They had a large front porch which extended across the front of the house and around part of the side. Green wicker chairs, tables with flowers and a swing graced the front porch. Main Street was beginning to become commercial with lots of traffic. By the time I joined the family, the porch was no longer a gathering place except on the Fourth of July when friends and neighbors gathered to watch the parade. People filled the chairs, swing and porch steps to watch the event of the summer. When the Fiddlers Convention was in town, we often sat on the porch to watch all the people coming and going.

Tom and I moved into a newly built house two days after we were married. The original plans included a patio at the back of the house. Because of the lay of the land, either six steps would have to be built from the kitchen door down to the ground, or the patio turned into a porch. We chose to have the patio converted to a porch with a cement floor and wrought iron railings. Sliding glass doors and the kitchen door opened onto the porch. The entrance to the porch from the driveway had two steps and side railings. The house also had a rather narrow front porch. We had some porch furniture for the back porch and a white wicker rocking chair for the front porch. The house did not have central air conditioning.

We were one of the first to move into this new development. Vacant lots were on either side of us. That soon changed. Our first summer there, we watched houses being built on either side as we grilled out and ate supper on the back porch. By the end of summer, we had friendly neighbors with children all around us. As friendships grew, and children were born, I often sat on the front steps with another mother and watched the children play. Later, the children played in the back yards. Ours was a baseball field and another had a tree house. A roof was added and the cement porch became a screened porch. The children grew older and the porch became a summer activity room. The children went off to college and the porch was glassed in and became the sunroom. From then on, the sunroom became our family room. Tom ate all his meals there. I ate lunch and supper there. I could watch the neighbors come and go as well as the birds at the two bird feeders, the squirrels, chipmunks and deer. When Tom was dying, he wanted to be in the sunroom; so that is where we placed the hospital bed and that is where he died.

On my first visit to Happy Home, I was greeted by two gentlemen sitting in rocking chairs on the porch. My daughter told me later: "You always enjoy talking with men. You will enjoy rocking and talking on the porch." And, so I have. When I first moved here there were three rocking chairs on one side of the Club House front porch and four on the other side. Now, because of COVID-19 there are only two chairs six feet apart on either side. Nevertheless it is a welcoming space, even if no one else is on the porch. There are always birds chirping or trees blowing or something moving. Usually someone is sitting in a favorite chair. The warm feelings of being with others seem to spread over those sitting in chairs or on nearby benches. Some even sit on their rollators. People do try to stay six feet apart. People are not sitting on the porch to escape a hot apartment but to enjoy fresh air and companionship and to watch whatever might be going on in the neighborhood, be it people, cars, animals, birds, trees or flowers. Porches resonate the warm feelings of peace with others and the world in general.

The Parking Lot

I walk around and around the parking lot and wonder if anyone is watching me and if they are thinking "Here she comes again." The parking lot is at the top of a rather long incline. It is a rectangular lot which serves two apartment buildings. One of the long sides is a buffer area of green grass and tall trees. Behind the trees is a city road. On the opposite side is an apartment building shaped like an L. That building extends almost to the second building which is opposite the wide entrance to the parking lot. In the middle of the lot is an oblong grassy area with two shade trees. Parking spaces are marked off along the three sides of the lot. The lot is relatively flat, has several sidewalks going into various doors of the buildings and has three benches close to the sidewalks.

I live on the third floor of the L-shaped building. I can see only a small part of the parking lot from my windows. One day I saw a couple walking in the lot and thought "That might be a nice place to walk." I had never ventured down to that lot. Since then, I've learned about the entrances into the buildings and how the buildings are actually connected by an underground walkway.

It is an interesting walk. The birds are chirping, the sun shining, the breeze is cooling and the tall trees are reducing the road noises. I can hear and see nature while knowing I am in the real world.

Many times when I've been walking I would see someone or hear a car door slam and then never see where they went. They just disappeared in thin air. What I didn't realize was that most people who park in this lot use the end doors to come and go. They park right in front of the door. People who live on the second floor of my building can enter and exit the building without having to use the elevator.

One day I noticed that a rolled-up rug was being dropped from a third-floor window. Then various items were thrown out the window. I was amazed at how all the various items, even parts of a kitchen sink, fell in the same place, never hitting the building or the nearby tomato plant. I had on previous occasions watched workmen going in and out ground level apartment windows. Sometimes windows are an efficient way of moving people, supplies and trash in and out of buildings.

Since walking in the parking lot, I've discovered many different things. Next to my building are three large pots of yellow rose bushes just beginning to bloom. At the side of an entrance to another building is a small metal angel standing on a short pole. The angel is almost hidden by a rather large stone leaning against the building. On the stone is written "Stop and count your blessings." On the other side of the doorway is a ceramic brown rabbit. Not too far away from this building is a dog waste disposal. It has several different parts. I have not investigated it. In front of the opposite end of the same building is a series of white stone objects. One is a white dog sitting on its hind legs.

Another is just the rear of a dog, as though he was digging headfirst into the ground. Between the dogs is a group of three different hanging bird feeders, a bird bath and a hanging bird house.

I watch, ponder, imagine and then leave to walk in a different place, still looking for what's new in the neighborhood.

A Place to Live or Die

When I started looking for a new place to live, I was thinking about places where I would be able to enjoy my usual activities as well as a place I could take planned trips and new adventures — a place to live and enjoy the good life. That is what I bought into but I must admit, I was surprised at the number of residents older than I am. Yet and again, it is a retirement community.

When the COVID-19 virus and its impact hit in March, life as I had anticipated quickly came to a halt . here and across the nation. My eyes are seeing a different life. Instead of a place to live, I've chosen a place to die. I have no other place to go. The bright sunny apartment is a semi jail for now. I can walk outside in "nice" weather. I can drive my own car. Both of those activities depend on my good health. Food no longer tastes particularly good. I eat because it is something to do and is necessary for energy. What pleasure is food if eaten alone?

My children come to see me, but I can't touch them or hug them or share a meal with them. They have their own lives and their own difficulties with the virus and its limitations. I am alone in three rooms and two bathrooms. Around me are others in the same situation. I see them in the halls and speak with them but that is all. There is no "in- apartment visiting."

Yes, I know I have many blessings. My children do not have to worry about me or check on me twice a day. I have the necessities of everyday life but, this is the place I will die. Tom wanted to die at home and he did. I've never thought of where I wanted to die. That thought had never been in my mind or consideration. Now it is. Recently when I was sitting on the porch, rocking with the old folks, an ambulance pulled in the driveway. The question of the day is "Are they bringing someone back or taking someone away?"

The Church Parking Lot

Knollwood Baptist Church is a friendly, community-minded church. From its earliest beginnings, it has allowed many various community groups to use its facilities. The parking lots overflow with cars for the weekly Sunday services and other church events. During the week, cars come and go with parents bringing young children to preschool classes, adults coming for church or community meetings, others coming to enjoy the gym or walking track and teenagers coming for pickup basketball games. The parking lot always has parked cars: morning, noon and sometimes even at night.

One Saturday, after five weeks of the COVID-19 lock down, my daughter Lisa suggested we meet at the church parking lot and visit. I am living in a retirement community and family members are not allowed on campus except to bring food or prescription drugs which are to be left at the reception desk. The plan was that Lisa would bring a folding chair and I could sit on one of the benches near the main parking lot. This way we could be six feet apart and sit outdoors under shade trees and enjoy ourselves. On my drive to the church, I laughed at myself remembering that I was going to meet my daughter in the same parking lot in which, many years ago my deceased husband and I would "park." That was when the educational building was under construction. It was a safe place to be then and a safe place now.

We were not the only ones in the parking lot that sunny afternoon. Before Lisa arrived, a man pulled his van into a different part of the lot, parked, opened the rear door and out came a leashed dog ready for a nice long walk. After 45 minutes or so, they returned. The man put the dog in the van and off they went.

Meantime, a young girl learning to ride a scooter appeared with, I assume her mother driving what looked like a small, lightweight red golf cart. They went around the smaller of the parking lots several times. The girl on the scooter was having a hard time. Soon they disappeared. Later they returned both riding in the cart. Then what appeared to be two teenagers arrived in the same cart. They went around and around every place one could go around several times. They left and returned with the passenger stretched out with feet on the front of the cart. Around and around they went. Obviously, a fun time was being had.

A little later, an older looking man pulled up across from us, parked his car, opened the trunk and pulled out a bicycle and air pump. He pumped up a tire, put on his helmet and rode off. Lisa said he wasn't a regular biker as he had on shorts and the wrong kind of shoes. His car was still there when we left an hour later.

The mailman also made a visit to the parking lot. He didn't deliver any mail but parked in the shade near Knollwood Street. We wondered what he was doing: sorting mail, eating or just taking a break. Several cars and trucks used the parking lot entrance in which to turn around.

The KBC parking lot was a wonderful place to spend time with my daughter. I could see the glistening white steeple in the clear blue sky, hear the birds chirping, watch the graceful tree limbs sway in the breeze and feel the small brown bugs crawl up my arms. I could visit with my daughter while watching the world go by and know that God was close.

Sixty Days

I've had to eat alone in my apartment for 60 days and have had little face-to-face interaction with others. Activities came to a screeching halt on March 17, 2020. I walk alone outside for 30 minutes each day, read my daily devotion books, keep a diary, play computer bridge and sometime sit on the porch and watch the baby birds in their nest. The trip to the mailbox is the highlight of the day. Will there be something in the box? Sometimes it is empty, not even a charity letter asking for money. Today there was a postcard from the newly hired WFU basketball coach wanting me to buy tickets for the 2020 -2021 season. (There may not even be a 2020-2021 college basketball season.) This certainly is not the life the Happy Home Retirement Community advertised.

Looking on the bright side of my situation in the COVID-19 pandemic, I have a place to live and food to eat, a TV to watch, a computer to keep in contact with the world as well as the daily newspaper delivered to my door. The newspaper may be only a few pages but I read almost every word while eating breakfast. Somehow the days seem to pass and the world continues to go around and around.

I've finally learn to manage a mask with my hearing aids, glasses and wig all behind my ears. That's been a real trick. People may wonder why my hair isn't turning gray or growing longer. That's for me to know and them to guess. The big thing that keeps me balanced is having a car. I can drive away from the Happy Jail if the car needs some exercise or if I need to go somewhere. The car and I have visited the drive-through window at the bank and at CVS. Because visitors are not allowed at the Happy Jail, several times I've met one of my children in the parking lot at Knollwood Baptist Church. We sit six feet apart on benches underneath a lovely shade tree and visit.

This afternoon I sit and ponder over the things I've seen as I've walked around and around the parking lot. Recently I realized that instead of two yellow rose bushes at the corner of my building there are three. The bushes are in cement containers and were planted and cared for by a second-floor resident. The roses can be seen from his apartment windows. The nearby empty plant stand also belongs to the resident and he plans to plant a begonia in it later this spring. I continue to check on the status of the pumpkin not far from the yellow roses and the leftover Christmas poinsettia on a different walkway.

The other day, I noticed a resident who had appeared out of nowhere standing close to a large container which was not next to a walkway. I asked him what was in the container and much to my surprise, it was two tomato plants. If he has a big crop, I hope he will share.

Yesterday when I was walking, I noticed a second dog waste disposal contraption in the grassy area in the middle of the parking lot. A maintenance man was cleaning it out and replacing supplies. Today right in front of me, a chipmunk scampered across the sidewalk and up a six foot brick embankment.

People still appear and disappear, cars come and go, but I'm beginning to know where to watch and listen for doors to open and shut. After sixty days, I am beginning to accept the repetition of life.

Grocery Store Adventure

After 13 weeks of not being in a public place, I decided that today, June 18, 2020, I would go to the grocery store. Living in a retirement community, I need only a few groceries. My family and friends had "picked up" for me most of what I had needed. Today was my big day. Last night I studied the weekly grocery store ads and checked out my coupons. Then I made my list. It was not long.

Sprinkles had interrupted my morning walk. So, I decided to wear my 30-year-old long beige raincoat. After removing the coat's lining, I gathered together all the paraphernalia I would need and headed off to my car. As soon as I got to the car, I remembered I had not put my cell phone in my pocketbook, so I had to reenter the building, ride the elevator up to the third floor, get the phone and return to the car. When I got to the entrance gates of the "Happy Jail," it started to rain. All the way to the grocery it rained but miraculously let up as I pulled into the parking lot.

There were several empty parking spaces, two of which were "drive through." Unfortunately, I was not quick enough to get through one as a car coming from the other side, pulled in first. At the second space, I was at a bad angle to get in and blocked traffic trying to reverse. I drove around the lot once again and finally parked behind a car. Enough is enough.

After parking, I put on my mask, being very careful not to get my glasses, hearing aid, nor wig caught in the elastic ties to the mask. Then I put the handles to my pocketbook over one shoulder and my beige Warthog hat with the wide brim on my head.

Once inside the store, an employee was wiping down the handles of the carts and handed me one. I noticed neither one-way signs nor any 6 feet markers. The employees were wearing gloves and I think masks. What I did notice was so many shelves with vacant spaces. I would have gotten some toilet paper but the "pickings were few and far between." I got the important items (candy, cookies, ice cream sandwiches) on my list and all but two of the remaining items.

Check out was quick and efficient. I asked for help. A guy who looked to be an older teenager carried my four bags to the car. I wasn't certain exactly where I had parked but he asked for the make and color of the car and spotted it immediately. Because he was carrying the bags and not pushing a cart, he just cut through the parked cars straight to mine. As soon as I got in the car, I took the mask off without catching a hearing aid. Upon arrival home, I was able to get the groceries into the building and up to my apartment without dropping a thing. Mission accomplished— food and a trip out into the world.

Memories of a Beloved Companion

Billy my big brother, Walter my little brother and I had a dearly beloved companion. He was always getting into trouble just like Billy. He, however, never got caught; always escaping punishment by the hair on his chinny, chin, chin. We never saw our hero but we knew what he looked like. We didn't know exactly where he lived but we knew it was close by. He had many friends. Billy knew them all. His name was Billy Goat Pete.

Billy Goat Pete came into our lives after our father died and we had moved to Charleston, WV to live with my mother's parents. Bedtime was our special time alone with mother. She would read us stories as well as tell us stories of the adventures of Billy Goat Pete. I always loved hearing about Billy Goat Pete. When my children were young and mother came to visit, somehow, to the delight of the children, Billy Goat Pete found his way to our backyard.

Recently I found a file of Billy Goat Pete stories mother had written to Walter in the summer of 1947, the first year he was at Camp John Lang. Walter was eight years old and may not have wanted to go to camp. Mother felt he needed to be able to play with boys his own age. There were not any little boys for Walter to play with in our neighborhood. Following is one of those letters.

"Dear Walter. It is now 5:45 A.M. I came downstairs for the paper but Basil hadn't arrived with it. Or, if he passed it, Billy Goat Pete found it and ate it up. Do you suppose that is what happened?

He wandered up to Camp John Lang the other day. Some boys saw him down at the river and began teasing him. They came too close and pulled his whiskers. He didn't like this a bit so he just turned around and began butting them.

Before anyone knew what had happened, two were in the water, clothes and all. Did those boys ever shiver and shake! Two others ran for the counselor but he had arrived with a bunch of carrots for the goat. Billy Goat Pete ate the carrots and let the counselor lead him back to his home about a mile down the road. Then all the boys began to make craft work as it began to rain.

Billy goats have an awful smell and are usually dirty for they never bathe very well. If Billy Goat Pete wanders into camp, do you suppose the boys in your cabin can take him down to the river and bathe him? He would have to be tied first and a whole box of soapsuds used on him. Wouldn't he be funny looking with soapsuds all over him?

Lots of love, Mother"

About ten years before she died, Mother moved into an apartment building high on a hill overlooking the

61

river and city. Several weeks after mother's death, I closed her apartment door for the final time and drove down the steep winding road. It was then that I saw Billy Goat Pete for the first and only time. He wore a small cow bell on a red leather strap around his neck. As he saw me, he shook his head from side to side ringing his bell, kicked up his heels and waved me a good-bye kiss. A lifetime memory!

Will I Survive

Will I survive my decision in 2019 to move from my home of 55 years to the Happy Home Retirement Community? I had been involved in a variety of activities: playing bridge three afternoons a week, going to church twice a week, attending a writing group monthly, walking with neighbors daily and lots of other social activities. The decision had not been extremely difficult to make. The house had developed problems as had the yard. (It was a $1000 here, a $1000 there.) Arthritis in my back prohibited me from working in the yard. Although I had yard service, no one could keep the yard the way I had. Eight months earlier I had been hospitalized because of a fall in the yard. It was time to move on to a different life.

Gradually I began to incorporate some of the Happy Home activities into my life. The various people I ate supper with were friendly and interesting. I spent Thanksgiving and Christmas with my daughter and her family as my son had recently moved to Virginia. Life was moving along smoothly. Then, COVID-19 hit North Carolina and on March 17, 2020, the governor shut down the state. The Happy Home Retirement Community became the Happy Jail. The dining room and café were closed. Meals could be ordered and delivered to residents. All activities were cancelled. No outside visitors were allowed on campus. Visiting inside the apartments or cottages was not allowed but we could leave the campus for essential reasons. Then came the mask wearing and six feet apart rules. The "shutdown" was supposed to be for several weeks but several weeks were extended and re-extended.

By the sixtieth day I was "at the end of my rope." Each day for thirty minutes I walked around and around the back parking lot often talking to God. Once I asked him "How long are we going to have to deal with COVID-19" and, at the same time, I thanked him for a safe place to live, food to eat and the ability to at least see a few people. I always ended my walks at the front entrance to the Club House. Usually someone would be sitting in one of the four rocking chairs on the porch. The chairs, of course, were six feet apart. I always stopped to chat a few minutes, after first putting on my mask.

In the back parking lot there were things to watch: workmen coming and going, birds, squirrels, chipmunks, tomato plants growing and a yellow rose bush beginning to bud. Inside my apartment I had several daily devotion books to read, a diary to record daily happenings, a TV to watch and a computer on which I could play bridge with my longtime partner. We played bridge every night for two hours. The trip to the mailroom was the excitement of the day. Would there be a note or card or even a bill waiting for me?

Eventually the Governor relaxed some of the restrictions and we were allowed to eat in the dining room but fewer people at a time and only four people to a table. I was elated to be able to eat supper with other people. As the weeks and months have gone by, the rules and regulations have increasingly lessened. Gradually more activities have been added to the social calendar but always the rules of six feet apart, masks and limited number of participants have remained in place. Last week we were allowed to have outside visitors in the apartments but not in the dining room or other inside areas of the campus.

COVID-19 has affected my emotional health. My nerves are shot. Any little problem throws me into a tizzy. When will it ever be over? Computer and cell phones glitches seem to be insurmountable. Even though I've seen my children almost weekly, outside in the church parking lot six feet apart, I've not been able to touch them nor to see their unmasked faces. Last weekend both children visited me in the apartment...six feet apart and wearing masks. Instead of joy, I felt detachment. It was almost like entertaining a stranger in my home. Texting, e-mails and phone calls just don't adequately convey deep down feelings and after a while, the feelings just seem to vanish into thin air. Emotional detachment from my children is a terrible feeling. I feel like I'm alone in the world. Am I really going to survive this? Tomorrow, when I walk around and around the parking lot, I'll talk to God about my feelings and look for a message in the wonderful world of nature.

The Pumpkin

I first noticed the pumpkin early this spring when I discovered the flat parking lot close to the building in which I live. I can see only a small part of the parking lot from the windows in my third-floor apartment. Located between two apartment buildings and used by only a few residents, it is a great place to begin my morning walk. In addition to the sidewalks around the parking lot, are two long sidewalks to side doors. The trees are full of birds. Chipmunks and squirrels scamper across the well-maintained green grass. The residents have made the area their own with various bird feeders, bird houses, a bird bath and large containers of flowers, rose bushes, even tomato plants. There is always something different to see and watch.

I had walked the lot several times before I noticed the deep orange, almost brown pumpkin. Located near a corner of my building, it was surrounded by pine needles and behind some small shrubs. The slightly curved stem made it perfect for a fall front porch decoration. I kept wondering who would have put a pumpkin in such a remote place and was it real or ceramic. After weeks of walking by and watching the pumpkin from a distance, I walked across the grass and thumped it lightly. Nothing happened. I did not want to hit it hard. If it was real, it would be rotten and squash all over the place; if ceramic, it could break. So, I let it be and continued to watch.

66

Several weeks later, the answer was obvious. The stem was not as high above the pine needles as it had been. The next week it was lower in the pine needles but perfectly shaped. Gradually it got lower and lower. Then it just sank into the ground, the top and stem still perfectly shaped. June 5th I walked over the grass to take a closer look. The top had cracked a bit but the perfectly shaped stem stood tall. The pumpkin was just below the pine needles. It must have rotted all the way from the bottom up with the seeds now deep in the ground. I wonder if there will be a pumpkin crop this fall in time for Halloween. I'll keep watching.

The Toilet Paper Olympics

Wednesday, August 26, 2020, was a day in history: the world's first Toilet Paper Olympics. This exciting event was held in the Club House of the Happy Home Retirement Community. Because of the pandemic, the event was limited to twelve enthusiastic, athletically talented contestants. Of those participating, one was in a wheelchair, one used a walker, one rode on a motor scooter, one had difficulty understanding directions and one was a petite 94-year-old lady. Everyone wore a mask.

The room was arranged with six tabletop stations. The sixth was a sit-out station. The events of the day were Toilet Paper Hockey, Toilet Paper Basketball, Toilet Paper Miniature Basketball, Toilet Paper Baseball, and Toilet Paper Memory. We played in groups of three.

Toilet Paper Hockey is played with the spindle of a toilet paper holder as the hockey stick. The puck was tape folded to make somewhat of a ball. The goal consisted of a strip of toilet paper held together at each end by a roll of toilet paper. To play, one pulled back on the spring of the spindle, releasing the power to move the puck. Not an easy task with weak arthritic hands and fingers. When successful, it is fun to watch the puck fly across the field.

Toilet Paper Basketball is a much easier game. The leader holds up a large hula hoop and the contestant is given ten rolls of toilet paper to throw through the hoop. The expert at this game threw the rolls in the hoop while standing backwards.

Toilet Paper Miniature Basketball is played with tape balls and a pyramid of three rolls of toilet paper. The player is given ten balls and tries to throw each ball in the hole of the top roll of toilet paper. This is a challenge!

Toilet Paper Baseball is a little different. This time a contestant is given ten rolls of toilet paper and tries to throw each roll so that it lands standing up.

Memory Toilet Paper is a game consisting of ten rolls of toilet paper standing up. Inside each roll is a colored stick. The ten sticks are divided into five different colors. The referee places the sticks in the various rolls and covers each roll with a hat. The first person picks two rolls. If the colors don't match, the hats are placed back on the rolls and the next person picks two rolls. When a player picks a match, the player keeps his sticks. The game is played until all the sticks have been matched.

When the laughter had settled down and everyone had played all five games, each person was given three rolls of toilet paper to take home. It was a different and fun way to spend an hour. The prizes were precious considering the toilet paper shortage during the pandemic.

Thursday

The day was Thursday, September 9, 2020, Senior Citizen Day with 5% off at Harris Teeter. The sky was overcast. The moisture on the outside of the windowpanes indicated high humidity. Looking out the window, the sidewalks appeared to be dry. I dressed for my usual walk and headed out the apartment building. I could not see any moisture falling from the sky but I could feel wet on my legs. My lightweight rain jacket did not show any signs of being wet. A rather dark cloud did appear overhead but seemed to be moving away. My legs got wetter and my body felt damp. So, I gave up on my walk and returned to the building by way of the front porch of the Club House and chatted with several folks sitting in the rocking chairs enjoying their morning visits. Then I got a cup of coffee and returned to my apartment to fix breakfast.

My plan for the day was to go to the bank, transfer money to pay taxes and get cash to reimburse Barbara for my bridge games, go to Barbara's, stop by the church to pick up a communion packet for the Sunday service and on to Harris Teeter. By now, the mist had stopped but the sky was gray. Nevertheless, I carried my raincoat and hat, pocketbook with check book, grocery list and coupons, my large thermos bag, two cloth grocery bags, face mask and car keys as I headed out to accomplish my chores.

The trip to the bank was uneventful although I did have to show my driver's license and sign the withdrawal slip. No cars were behind me in the drive-through lane, so I didn't have to hurry to count my money. (My mother taught me to always count my money before leaving the counter.) Then it was off to Barbara's. I'd been to Barbara's several times and knew exactly how to get there until I saw the "road closed" sign. I turned to the right at the next right and "followed my nose" until ending up at the "road closed" sign again. By then I had a plan and was able to find my way to Barbara's driveway. A car was parked close to the house in the turnaround area. I just stopped and parked in the middle of the driveway. Barbara met me at the door in her wheelchair as she is recovering from a broken ankle. I thanked her for paying my bridge fees, gave her the envelope and returned to the car. Although tricky, I was able to back out the driveway not hitting a tree nor running over any flowers. Because of the closed road I had to drive to Harris Teeter a different way and never got to the church to pick up my packet.

My shopping list was rather short. Only two items for the thermos bag: a quart of milk and two cups of yogurt, and several other items which were to go in the cloth bags. Harris Teeter does not allow the checkout clerks to bag customers' bags, so I told the clerk to bag mine in plastic bags. When I got to the car, I put the plastic bags in my cloth bags. The cloth bags and the thermos bag have long handles which I can put over my shoulders and therefore are much easier to carry. After getting the groceries in the car and the grocery cart back to its place, I studied my receipt. As I suspected, the milk and yogurt had not been included. I thought to myself: "If I don't go back and pay for those two items, I will surely have a wreck on the way home."

I marched back into the store and went to the customer service desk. I explained that the clerk had overlooked my milk and yogurt and I needed to pay for them. I had my receipt but there was a problem because the lady did not know the cost of the items. I told her what the prices were and she finally rang up a bill and I paid the additional $2.19 and returned to the car.

The car would not start. I could not move the gear shift. I pushed the start button and gas and break peddles several times. No combinations seem to work. Panic set in. I returned to the customer service desk and explained I needed help as my car wouldn't start. They looked at me with blank stares. The lady wanted to know if she could call someone for me as I looked sick. Finally one of the assistant mangers offered to go to the car with me. On the way, I wondered if I had pushed the correct start button. So I got in the car and sure enough I pushed a different button and the car started. The assistant manager had held the car door open for me and, before he closed it, he asked if I was ok. He must have thought: "What a crazy lady she is."

I did not have a wreck on the way home. Before getting out the car, I put my mask on and got my apartment key chain out of the pocketbook. Then I got the three bags of groceries and pocketbook over my shoulders and into the building, up the elevator and to my apartment. After putting the groceries away, I returned to the car, got my raincoat and hat, locked the car, decided to order the hotdog special for lunch and preceded to my mailbox. Only then did I realize I had left my apartment and mailbox keys in the apartment. So I had to go the concierge desk, get a master key, return to the apartment, get my keys, return the master key, get my mail from my post office box and wait for my hot dog order. By the time I got back to the apartment with my lunch and ate my hotdogs, I was completely exhausted and stayed in my apartment until supper time. Supper was good; online bridge with Barbara afterwards was not so good. What a day! What a day!!

Ash Wednesday

It was Wednesday, February 17, 2021, a cold and breezy day. Monday and Tuesday had been wet and cold. Freezing rain and ice were predicted for Thursday but on this day, Ash Wednesday, the sun was out and the sky was clear blue. I considered the weather a gift from above.

For many years Knollwood Baptist Church has had a noon Ash Wednesday service followed by a soup and bread lunch. Because of COVID-19, this year the service was an outdoor walk-through service in the Memorial Garden which adjoins the largest church parking lot. Folks could come and walk through any time between noon and 1:30 p.m. We were told to wear a mask and maintain social distance.

It was just noon when I drove into the parking lot. I was surprised at the number of cars already in the parking lot and thought that people must be waiting in their cars to take their turn to begin the walk. I found a close drive- through parking space and noticed several people at the desk near the entrance to the Memorial Garden. The parked cars were empty. I got out of the car, put my mask on and pulled the hood to my jacket up over my head. I did not recognize the lady at the desk who gave me the order of worship form and told me I could join the four people already inside the gate. Masks make it difficult to recognize anyone. The Memorial Garden is enclosed by a brick and wrought iron fence about five feet tall. Trees and shrubs on either side of the fence conceal three sides of the Garden. Inside, one can hear traffic but not see it.

Once inside we were greeted at the first station and read the opening prayer. Then we proceeded to where Dr. Setzer was standing under the archway to the upper part of the Garden. He led us in several prayers and then administered the imposition of ashes. I was a problem for Dr. Setzer. Between my mask, glasses and hood, there was little room for an ash cross. He asked me to remove my hood which I began to do but the hood caught my wig and was lifting the wig off my head. Quickly he said that if it was a problem he would be very careful. I imagine he is still laughing.

At the next station was a table covered with a white cloth on which were scattered a variety of rocks. The rocks represented our sins or actions we wanted to turn away from during Lent and afterwards. After prayerful thought, we each chose a rock and placed in it the bowl which was also on the table. Then Josh Godwin, using a pitcher, poured water over the stones. It was very moving to see my sins being washed away.

As we continued our uphill walk towards the fourth station, I stopped at The Wall of Ashes monument to read the names of those whose ashes had been spread nearby. As I was thinking that I was indeed on a trail of ashes, I arrived at the fourth station. Katherine Martin was giving the group instructions to look around and find something of nature to put in the wreath which was in the middle of the cloth covered table. This act represented our appreciation of nature and recognition that we are part of nature. I found an interesting looking stick. Also on the table were colored rectangular cards. On the cards were words of things we might want to improve or develop during Lent. We were to select a card and pin it on the small bulletin board standing next to the table. After reading scripture, we moved to the last station which was the benediction and dismissal by Rozanna Goocey.

The entire experience was thought provoking and meaningful. I felt enclosed in a space with God and fellow travelers on the same path towards heaven. I was in the world, doing worldly things, but had a feeling of being out of the world. Enclosed from the world, but hearing sounds of the world.

Unsolved Mystery

Saturday, February 20, 2021, was the day of an unsolved mystery at Happy Home Retirement Community. My daughter Lisa and I had tea at the Flower Box restaurant on Friday to celebrate my birthday. Son Tim wanted to celebrate the occasion with all the family but Lisa was concerned about being around people in a public place as my grandson Conner had not been vaccinated. So they agreed to all have lunch in my apartment on Saturday. Tim would bring the food. I got out my winter place mats and napkins. Lisa and Conner arrived and then Tim came with our orders from Panera Bread. We sat on the 200- year-old antique chairs at the round dining room table. This was the first time I had eaten at the table since moving to the apartment. We all enjoyed the fellowship and laughter.

Later in the afternoon we were all going to a baby shower for Sarah, Tim's daughter. Before leaving, I asked Tim to tighten the back of a kitchen chair and to carry my large peace lily plant to the kitchen sink for a good watering. He didn't water it exactly as I thought he should. Time was running short, so I had him carry the plant back to the antique wooden plant stand in the corner close to the dining room table. Then we left. Lisa and Conner drove in her car as they had to go home before going to the shower. I rode with Tim directly to Advance and the shower. Afterwards, I rode home with

Lisa and Conner. Conner drove as he had his learner's permit. I got out of the car in front of the apartment.

After hanging up my coat and putting away my pocketbook, I went over to the peace lily and felt around the dirt. I decided it needed more water. I went to the sink, filled a bottle with water and headed to the plant. Then I stopped in horror! There on the floor between the plant stand and dining room table was a dead mouse. I walked close to the mouse and it did not move. For sure, it was dead. It was so dead that dry mouse hair was on the green carpet. There was no sign of any type of injury or odor. Where did the mouse come from? What does one do with a dead mouse in the house? My first thought was to put it in the disposal. Then I remembered that, with any problem at the Happy Home, one calls the person at the concierge desk. So, I called the desk and reported a dead mouse in my apartment. The weekend person replied that she would call the weekend manager on duty. The manager sent a young assistant chef to the rescue. The chef arrived with glove-covered hands holding a small brown cupcake box. He scooped the mouse up into the box. Before leaving, he said the manager would be checking on the situation later. On Sunday, the manager came to check out exactly where the mouse had been. She said she would send a report to maintenance.

Now the question was and remains "How did the mouse get on the floor?" The ceiling heat vent is at the far end of the room. There are no openings in the room except for windows and doors. A live mouse would not have come into the room and then just dropped dead near the plant. The mouse had to have appeared between the time I left and returned. Otherwise one of us would have stepped on it when we were coming and going from the table. The large peace lily was sent to me when my husband died in July 2015. It came with me to the apartment in November 2019. The plant has been in the exact place ever since except for the two times it has been taken to the kitchen sink. The mystery remains: How did the mouse get in the house?

The Purple Awning

New experiences are often challenging: belly dancing was difficult but fun; ziplining was scary but manageable; cardiac rehab is overwhelming but has possibilities. After a three-night hospital stay and the placement of a stent in a 90% blockage of a main artery, I was referred to the hospital's cardiac rehabilitation program. The rehab program lasts for three months. Four weeks after leaving the hospital, I reported for my first session. The class meets three times per week. Two classes last an hour and fifteen minutes. The third class meets an additional thirty minutes for "education."

The first fifteen minutes are used to sign-in which involves various health tests before receiving a plastic bag with your name on it. In the bag are several items which a person might use each time. (At the end of each class those items used are returned in the bag.) Next, one gets a heart monitor. If the person has worn a shirt with a pocket, the monitor goes in the pocket and the three leads are attached to specific places on the chest. In the plastic bag is a blue cloth pocket to use if your shirt doesn't have a pocket. This blue pocket has a strap which goes around the neck to hold the pocket on your chest. After getting the heart monitor and leads in place, the heart rate is checked. Last, is the selection of the equipment to be used for the first half of exercising. Finally, we are told to begin.

After the first 28 minutes, an announcement is made and everyone moves to a different type machine. Right before the end of the second session, the leader calls "cool down time." Everyone slows down their activity until "stretch time" is called. Then the group stands for stretches and the class is over. Each person wipes down his or her machine and turns in their monitor after first taking off the stickers, puts things back in their plastic bag, puts their bag in the receiving box and leaves.

As of this writing, I have been to two classes. The first was exhausting, overwhelming and confusing. The confusion started before I even got to the building. I had called for directions but had been given directions which didn't sound correct. Several days before the first class, my daughter drove me to the hospital to find the door I was to enter. Later, I had my son take me as I still was unsure. After talking with the nurse who called me the day before class, all I was certain of was that the door I wanted was under the purple awning. Surely I could find a door with a purple awning.

I was to report fifteen minutes early for the first class. I had decided the smart thing to do was to use transportation provided by the Happy Home Retirement Community. We arrived at 9:28. The door under the purple awning was locked. I knew the door would not be unlocked until 9:30. The driver waited until 9:30 when the nurse opened the door and I walked in.

Susan, my nurse, greeted me and started the process by giving me my plastic bag. Then there was blood pressure, oxygen rate and heart rate to be taken as well as weight (without shoes) and height to be measured. Of course, papers had to be read and signed. All of which was done with various machines and in various places with other nurses moving machines and people around. The next was placement of the heart monitor. My shirt did not have a pocket so I had to use the blue one from the plastic bag. After the monitor was placed in the blue pocket, the leads had to go from my neck down under my camisole and shirt and then attached to my chest. If that wasn't enough, goggles went over my glasses. I was now ready for class. Picture, me, dressed in old khaki slacks and a long sleeve pullover knit shirt, wires coming out from under the neck of the shirt, a strap around my neck connected to a blue bag holding the monitor, mask, hearing aids, glasses and a shield over the glasses. The shield was held in place with plastic strips over my head. (Somehow my wig did not fly off.) Later on, because I was having trouble breathing with the mask, I was given a "plastic cup like thing" to go under the mask and over the nose and mouth. A picture to behold!

My first exercise was not on a machine but was to walk around "the track" for 29 minutes. The "track" which went around the entire room, was white with purple footprints, six feet apart. On one side was a line of bicycle machines with old men with flabby bellies trying to look like Superman. On the other side were different machines and some rows of chairs. Several other patients were walking "the track" but they were using walkers. There wasn't much room on the "track" to pass those using walkers. Each time around, I was supposed to click a clicker. Sometimes I remembered and sometimes I didn't. At the appropriate time, everyone wiped down his or her machine and moved to a different machine.

Susan came to me and had me use a machine that works the legs and arms. It is somewhat like a bicycle but low to the ground and has a high back. I was glad to sit. While everyone was exercising, the staff was pushing machines around taking different measurements and asking you to rate how hard you were working. There was constant motion. At last, "slow down time" then "stretch time" came and the end of the session! The machine had to be wiped down and my gear, except for the monitor, had to go back into the plastic bag. I had a hard time getting the stickers off my chest. The monitors are numbered and have to be returned at "the monitor desk." When it was all done, I asked Susan to please call for my ride, which she did. I did not have to wait long before my ride arrived. I was so exhausted that, when I got to my apartment, I had to sit down and pop open a can of Ginger Ale.

What a Day!

What a day, what a day, Friday, May 21, 2021, was! Nothing earth-shaking but worth remembering for its lesson taught. After a good night's sleep, I got up a little after 8:00, dressed and walked down the stairs to the parking lot. There I walked for about 25 minutes and then down the driveway to the Club House. The rocking chairs on the porch looked so inviting that I sat and rocked for a few minutes before taking my transportation request forms to the concierge's desk.

Afterwards I stopped by the café to pick up my breakfast bag of cereal, milk, banana and raspberry pastry. After fixing a cup of to-go coffee, I returned to the apartment. I ate my breakfast, took my morning medicines and started getting ready for the housekeeper who arrives at 10:30.

Getting ready for the housekeeper involves taking everything off the bathroom countertop, my dresser, two chest of drawers and all the tables in the living room. The housekeepers are not supposed to lift nor move objects on furniture. This avoids the possibility of things getting broken. I decided the bathroom floor mats needed to be washed so I put them in the washer just as the housekeeper arrived. Then I went into my study for devotional reading and journaling.

As soon as the housekeeper left, I started on my errands with a to-do list in hand. CVS was the first stop. There I needed to pick up my prescription for Eliquis, a bottle of Centrum Silver and some vitamin D3. The shelves were packed with CVS vitamins, but no Centrum Silver. I also couldn't find a small bottle of D3. At the prescription pick-up counter, I told the clerk I couldn't find any Centrum Silver. She found some for me. As the clerk was ringing up the purchase, I noticed an extra charge. The CVS records showed an additional prescription was due. I had a three-months supply for that at home. The clerk removed that prescription from my bag. My CVS card showed a 40% off coupon which was used against the Centrum Silver. With purchases in hand, I left CVS and headed to the bank.

My time was getting shorter. I had filled out the deposit slip and signed the check to be deposited so the transaction went quickly and smoothly. I inquired and learned that customers were now allowed inside the bank. Leaving the bank, I took a short cut to Harris Teeter. That was a mistake as it involved a detour. Once at Harris Teeter I had a choice of several drive- through parking places. Great. Lady Luck was with me. Or so I thought.

My grocery list was short: lemon juice, paper napkins, facial tissue, instant oatmeal and Nabisco cookies. Everything was on sale. I had trouble deciding which package of cookies was on sale as none of the packages were marked $2.77. I put the two different sizes in my buggy. On the way to the checkout counter, I stopped by the deli department and got a small package of chicken salad. At the checkout counter, I asked the cashier which cookies were on sale. She had to look up the size from the newspaper ad. It was the larger size but I found that hard to believe so I had her ring it up and show me. I told her I didn't want the smaller one. I paid, after putting the credit card in upside down and having to redo that. I found my car without trouble, put the groceries in the back seat and headed for home. Time was getting short. HH Jeopardy was at 1:00 and it was now after noon.

My bill was $14.04. I usually check my bill before leaving the grocery store, but had not this time. On the drive home, I started figuring the bill in my head. It wasn't coming out right so at the next stop light I reached over for my pocketbook to get the receipt and the pocketbook was not on the seat. I always put my pocketbook on the front seat. I thought surely I didn't leave it in the buggy in the parking lot. The first place I could pull over and stop was Bolten Park. The pocketbook was in the back seat with the groceries. With a sigh of relief, I drove on to Happy Home Retirement Community, parked and got the groceries to the apartment. I put the chicken salad and strawberries in the refrigerator, fixed a quick snack and was off to HH Jeopardy.

After HH Jeopardy was over, I got my mail and returned to the apartment to put it back together from the cleaning and to put the mats in the dryer. Then I fixed a bigger snack and sat down to read the paper and make a phone call. After supper I played bridge and went to bed. The bed felt so good! I usually put my eye drops in each eye, put the bottle on the bedside table and turn off the light. Not this night! An hour after putting the drops in my eyes, I woke up with the eye drop bottle in my hand, the light on and my knees straight up just the way they are every night when I use the drops. Lesson learned: don't over schedule my day. I don't hurry very well.

The Protesters

It is Thursday, June 25, 2021, and I have an appointment at the Black Phillips Smith Government Center at 2301 North Patterson Avenue, Winston-Salem, NC to receive my gold and bronze medals in the Silver Arts division of the Piedmont Plus 2021 Senior Games. My "pick-up time" is 11:05 a.m. at the drive-through water bill payment window. The senior adult recreation department is located in this rather small building. I have been to the building before and am somewhat familiar with the general area.

For several weeks there have been protests and demonstrations in various parts of the city. They started in the downtown business areas and over time spread out into most areas of the city. Several days ago there was a protest involving cars going only ten miles per hour on University Parkway (a major four lane, 45 mph road) which resulted in traffic coming to a stoppage at a major crossroad. Traffic was halted for over 30 minutes. The crossroad was on my way to the Black Phillips Smith building. Consequentially, I allowed extra time for my appointment.

As I was approaching the building, I noticed a group of people holding signs and waving their arms in the air. They were standing close to the building but on the other side from the parking lot. Protesters at the Black Phillips Smith building? That was all my nervous self needed! The parking lot is small but I have parked in it several times with no problems. I could see the drive-through window around the corner of the building. As I was wondering how I was supposed to get to the window from the parking lot, I spotted an opening but it wasn't an opening for cars, only for people walking. Horror of all horrors, I had to turn around in this small parking lot. After about five tries, I managed to get turned around and drive out to Patterson Avenue, turn on a side street and then back towards the drive-through window. By now, one of the "protesters" was trying to direct me close enough to the window to retrieve my awards. After getting my envelope containing the medals and my entries, Chuck Vestal, the recreation department representative who is responsible for Senior Games, had me stop for picture taking and an awards ceremony speech with all the "protesters" cheering, jumping, and waving a multitude of signs. It was a sight to behold! The "protesters" were city recreation employees.

As I was leaving, I thought I was turning onto Patterson Avenue but I was not. I quickly realized my mistake but could not ascertain where I was. After several turns and many blocks, I could see University Parkway and headed for it, only to turn the wrong way but I knew where I was. Fortunately I was able to return to my apartment without encountering any real protesters along the way.

The Chair

Many years ago, a good friend and I swapped chairs. The chair I got is a "lady size" recliner. Recliners nowadays are much larger. Sixteen years ago I had the chair reupholstered. The armchair covers are now worn and faded. The chair doesn't recline very well but it is just right for me. The arms are just the right height and softness; the back is firm but not too firm; the seat is soft but not too soft and just the correct height for my feet to touch the floor.

The chair sits at an angle in a corner of my computer room at Happy Home. On the right side of the chair is a small two-shelved stand. A Blenko glass pencil holder filled with two pencils and a pen sit on the top shelf along with my coffee cup. Daily devotional books and my spiral notebooks fill the bottom shelf. Between the chair and stand is a blue cloth bag in which are folders of my recent writings. On the left side are a floor lamp and a slender box which holds my writing class information and several legal size note pads. Next to the box is a footstool my mother made on top of which are two throws. (The room is cooler than the others in the apartment.) Most of the time my lapboard sits on top of the throws. The computer desk and printer/copier finish my writing area.

Every morning for the last twenty years I begin the day by sitting in my chair reading several daily devotional books and then writing comments in a spiral notebook. After which I write in another spiral notebook the happenings of the previous day. Sometimes it's a long account, sometimes short. Thus my mornings usually begin with an hour in the chair.

My stories are written in the chair. On a very few occasions I've written a story while sitting on the front porch. Until COVID-19 came, I always wrote my stories at night. Now I play Computer Bridge at night and write stories during the day. I sit in the chair and think about what I want to write. Then make notes of those thoughts and organize them in some way. The notes become a writing. Once done the writing goes on the computer to the printer/ copier. Then it's back to the chair for corrections and revisions.

Although I have a desk next to the stand, I do all my writings in the chair. Checks, birthday cards, Christmas cards, notes, etc. are all written in the chair. I do not use the chair for anything except to read, ponder and write. This faded old chair is very special to me and I'm not about to have it reupholstered.

The Global Warming Article

Several weeks ago, a member of the Happy Home Writers group wrote an article on global warming with which he wanted some editing help. His plan was to submit it to the Winston-Salem Journal for publication on the editorial page but he knew the article was too long to meet the Journal's qualifications. Not only was the article long but it was very technical. After asking many questions about the meaning of the technical words and the process those words described, I was finally able to understand what he was saying. In fact, I became very interested in global warming.

At the next meeting, John thanked us for our input and said that he had submitted the revised article and it had been accepted for publication. The question was when. The next Thursday, John still had not gotten word regarding when the article would appear. On Saturday John and his wife left for their mountain home for the summer.

The following Tuesday I was at a painting class and overheard a conversation about seeing John's article in the Saturday's paper. I could not believe my ears! I had looked faithfully every day for several weeks for that article. John had even promised to e-mail the group members when he heard the date. On Sunday I had taken two weeks of newspapers and a bag of small paper notes to the recycle bin.

As soon as I finished my sunset over the ocean painting, I returned to my apartment and quickly headed for the recycle room. The room is very small. Two blue recycle bins sit close together against the wall. The door to the room is very heavy. When opened, the door clears the corner of the first bin by only an inch. If the bin is not against the wall, the door does not fully open and one has to twist and turn to get in. The light switch is on the wall close to the door. When the overhead light is turned on, a loud noise also comes on. Once inside, I pulled the bin out from the wall. Otherwise, the lid to the bin will not stay up and falls on whatever is in the way. I didn't pull it far enough out and it fell on my arm. After pulling it out a little farther, I looked in. The bin was about three-fourths full. On top of the papers was a large bag of non-paper recycle stuff. I put that bag on the floor and then began the process of reaching in and hand by hand taking the papers out. I dug deeper and deeper finding lots of local and some out-of-state newspapers but no Saturday's Winston-Salem Journal. By now, my hands could hardly reach the papers. I became concerned that if I fell head long into the bin I would be in a fix and no one would hear me. Even if I was able to wiggle and get upright, I would not be able to get out of the bin. Luckily, I found the Saturday Winston-Salem Journal's editorial section. I then put the papers I had taken out and the bag of assorted recycles back into the bin, pulled the lid down, put the bin against the wall, turned off the light and left.

Back in the apartment, I read the article. This time I could understand it. The article has made me rethink global warming, the problems it is causing and the realization that each of us has a part in reducing it.

The Delta Arts Center Adventure

My first "adventure" since the COVID-19 shut down was Friday, June 4, 2021. Martha, a dear friend, had invited Barbara my bridge partner and me to lunch and afterwards to attend a program and exhibit by Diane Britton Durham at the Delta Arts Center. Martha served us a delicious lunch on her long narrow porch overlooking the woods. We listened to the birds sing and watched the squirrels scamper as we ate and chatted. After lunch I read aloud several of my stories which had been winners in the Silver Arts division of the Senior Games. Barbara was unable to attend the art exhibit as she had to baby sit her grandchildren.

The Delta Arts Center which hosts various art exhibits and other community events is located in East Winston. I had visited previous events at the center but Martha had not. She was familiar with the area because she had volunteered at the Community Health Center and tutored at one of the area's Title 1 schools. We had no trouble finding the center.

The opening of the exhibit had been Thursday night. This afternoon, Ms. Durham gave an hour-long live presentation which was also zoomed. She is internationally known for her Gullah art. She has said that "her love of history and culture is the fuel that keeps her creating as well as helping others in the community discover their own creative passions." After her presentation, we spent time looking closely at

95

her works on display. I loved her paintings! Each picture was full of life and movement. The colors were bright, the figures distinct. It was interesting that none of the people had faces. The artist told me that she left the facial expressions up to the imagination of each viewer.

After enjoying the exhibit, we drove to a bus shelter farther east on the New Walkertown Road. Martha was instrumental in getting the Winston-Salem Public Art Commission to sponsor a project to increase the aesthetic appeal of city bus shelters and to improve the transit experience for riders. Seventy-five local artists had submitted proposals. Twelve were selected for the project. Each piece was transferred to clear vinyl and then attached to the inside of a bus shelter. Of the twelve, only the one at the New Walkertown Road shelter had been vandalized. Martha wanted to see the damage. On the way home she drove by the Rupert Bell Recreation Center to show me where she had won the gold medal for shuffleboard in the Senior Games. Clearly my friend has stayed busy during the pandemic!

It was a delightful, informative, and interesting afternoon adventure.

The Black Mountain Chocolate Factory

By July 2021 most of the COVID-19 restrictions had been lifted at Happy Home and life was almost back to normal. Off campus events resumed. July 7th was the first time in sixteen months that I had ridden on the Happy Home bus. The trip was to the Black Mountain Chocolate Factory, which is not located in Black Mountain but in the Innovation Quarter in Winston-Salem. Only seven passengers were on the bus, two of whom had not actually moved on campus.

The bus driver used a GPS for directions. I saw roads I'd never seen before. Looking out the window, all I saw was green grass, trees and roads, no buildings, houses nor peoples. Eventually we arrived at the Innovation Quarter area. Here I saw narrow streets, buildings, cars, trucks and people. The two-way streets were so narrow that our small bus was too long to park on the street.

Because parking was a problem, the driver had us get off the bus across the street from the factory and wait for her to park the bus. I spotted several chairs under an umbrella and headed straight for them. The chairs were close to a large open-air park. Several others joined me. It was hot standing on the sidewalk. We noticed that the bus went around the block several times. Eventually, the driver returned; we crossed the busy street and entered the chocolate factory.

The inside is long and narrow. One side faces an outside plaza. A few small round tables and chairs face the windows. On the opposite side is a long counter and bar. We were greeted by the host and asked to sit at the far end of the bar. The bar stools were high. (A requirement to attend this trip was to be able to get on and off high bar stools.) The host stood behind the bar to explain how and where chocolate is grown and the process of getting the chocolate bean to the solid chocolate we eat. After the lecture we were led to a window where we could see some of the process from start to finish.

What impressed me most was seeing the fruit of the chocolate plant. The fruit is the same shape as a small acorn squash. When cut, the seeds are the size and shape of squash seeds. Inside the seed is the small chocolate bean. The bean has a thin covering, similar to that of a peanut. That covering is eventually removed before the actual beginning of the chocolate making. Natural chocolate has different flavors depending on where it is grown and which plants are nearby. The Black Mountain Chocolate Factory buys all its chocolate from the Dominion Republic. From the chocolate field to the chocolate candy bar is a long process.

After being shown parts of the process, we returned to our seats at the bar. We were taught the proper way to eat chocolate. The first bite should be eaten slowly with the two front teeth gradually moving it around the mouth to get the full flavor of the chocolate. The tour ended with our tasting samples from six different flavored chocolate bars. While we were there, customers came and went with different chocolate drinks and other chocolate goodies. Some stayed and visited at the tables and chairs. Before leaving, I bought two boxes of candy for special gifts. Just as interesting as learning about chocolate was seeing part of the Innovation Quarter. Hopefully one day we will have a tour of the entire area. A good time was had by all.

The Ladder

I pass the ladder almost every day when I walk the halls for exercise. The ladder lends against the doorway of an apartment. Or the other side of the doorway is a small table. Usually a vase of flowers is on the table and often flowers are under the ladder. I learned that this handmade wooden ladder was recovered from a 250-year-old tobacco barn. It has aged well. The five rungs are flat. A delightful couple live in the apartment. One night at supper, I asked them why nothing was sitting on the ladder. The next day an empty bird nest appeared on the third rung. I happened to see the couple that night and asked where was the bird. The next day a chicken was in the nest. Each day something was added and each night at supper I asked to see more.

Day 3: the chicken looked like it was sitting on broken eggshells. Day 4: three chickens were in the nest. Day 5: one of the chickens was out of the nest sitting on the rung. Day 6: the nest was empty. Day 7: a cat was sitting in the nest. Seeing this distressed me and I had to express my feeling to the couple. Day 8: the chickens were back in the nest but looked rather dead. Day 9: the cat was hanging by a thread from the rung above. Day 10: the mother chicken was back in the nest; the chickens outside of the nest. Day 11: all the chickens, with the large one in the rear, were moving towards flowers at the end of the rung. Day 12: no chickens, just an empty nest. Day 13: the grieving mother hen was dressed in a black cape and moving towards the flowers. A sad day indeed. Day 14: a beautiful green origami was hanging above the empty rung. The crane was carrying the birds' souls to paradise. The life cycle of the chicken was over. But that was not the end of the story.

The next day a dinosaur was sitting in the nest. Day 16: a different dinosaur occupied the nest. Time passes slowly. Day 17: just an empty nest. How could my friends do this to me? What was going to encourage me to keep walking? When I voiced my complaint, I learned I had overlooked the beginning of the next story.

Day 18; I found the tiny butterfly eggs on a plant on the floor beside the ladder. I had not looked that closely the previous day. Day 19: there was a caterpillar around one of the leaves of the plant. Day 20: I spied several small green chrysalises. Day 21: small butterflies were on the plant and ladder. Day 22: I almost missed the lovely brown mental large butterflies. They had their wings close to their bodies and stood close to the ladder's sides. Day 23: lovely large fall-colored leaves hung all over the ladder. Day 24: hanging from the top rung was a small cut-out paper box. Day 25: a light was shining from within the box. Could that be the Church of the Animals? Day 26: on the table was a small ceramic monkey which appeared to be attached to something but the something was covered with white material. Day 27: revealed a second monkey. Day 28: the third monkey was uncovered. Under the monkeys was a note addressed to me. It read: "Old Chinese proverb: Speak no evil, see no evil, hear no evil." When I looked closely, one monkey had his eyes covered, one his ears covered, and one his mouth shut. What do you think my friends were telling me? Day 29 should be interesting.

Getting Gas

One would think that, after using self-service gas stations for twenty years, I could fill my car with gas all by myself. But, oh no, not this time.

It was 11:30 a.m. in late November 2020. The station was not crowded although there was a cleaning crew hosing down the area. I wondered why but assumed it was a usual cleaning. As luck would have it, I was able to pull in at the front of two tanks on the correct side of my car. I got out of the car, without knocking the door into the tank, proceeded to put the credit card in the correct slot and remove it as instructed. Then the notice said to "Enter card." So, I rechecked the picture on the directions, and re-entered the card. Once again," Remove card." "Enter card." I turned the card a different way and got the same answer. It was obvious the machine and I were having a problem. Since the hosing crew was still around, I motioned to the one man who appeared to be doing nothing. He came over and inserted the card. Bingo! It worked. Following instructions, I lifted the hose, pushed the button for regular gas, carried the hose to the gas tank door (which I had successfully opened) and then realized the gas hose would not reach to the gas tank. So I carefully laid down the gas hose, got in the car, prayed before starting the engine that I would not cause an explosion, started the engine and drove forward. I got out of the car, picked up the gas hose and filled the tank. I shut the gas tank door, hung up the hose, pushed the button to get a receipt and nothing happened. After waiting a long time, I went inside the station to get a receipt. Several people were standing around as if in a line six feet apart but not actually a line. Not wanting to cause trouble, I asked if they were in line. They were. Finally a second clerk came to help and asked if I had been at station three and needed help. (I had pushed the "help" button at the gas pump number three.) I told her the machine would not give me my receipt. She apologized and gave me a receipt. I successfully left the gas station and made my way home.

The next time I went to get gas, the credit card would not work. This time I asked a man at the next pump to help me. Once again the card worked. The third time I tried to get gas, the credit card was not acceptable to the pump. This time, I went inside the gas station and asked for help. I thought an employee would feel sorry for "the little old lady" and come out to the pump. But no, I could pay in advance for how many gallons of gas I wanted. Just as if I knew how much gas I needed. I paid for $20 worth of gas. Of course, $20 didn't fill the tank. The next and last time I needed gas, I had my son ride to the station with me. He had no problem with the credit card. (He did have a problem with my driving skills.) I will soon need gas. Maybe I should try a different gas station.

Recent Trips

During late summer and early fall I have learned several new facts mostly historical but some useful. On a tour of Historic Bethabara Park, I saw and felt the straw thread used to weave linen cloth. Now I better understand why I don't enjoy wearing linen clothes and why they are so hard to iron. It was worth tramping through the wet, uneven grass to learn this information.

On a second Happy Home trip to Mt. Airy, we took the Mayberry Squad Car Tour. The group rode in three separate cars with a guide. Each car was a replica of the Mayberry squad car. The tour began with the siren blasting. During the ride I acquired some interesting information about the Andy Griffin Show. Only Ford-made cars were allowed on the show. The reason being that Ford agreed to supply, free of charge, the police cars if no other make of cars was ever shown on the program. Ford provided the cars, painted them black, installed the sirens and delivered them to the set. Ever year or two when the cars were replaced, Ford repainted the cars and removed the sirens before selling them. I also learned that Andy ate hot dogs and not pork chop sandwiches at Snappy's. What really impressed me about Mt. Airy was the large granite quarry. It is the largest open-faced granite quarry in the world. I didn't know that the granite in the churches and other building in this area had been dug and cut nearby. The tour ended near Andy's office and jail. We had pictures made sitting in the jail cell. I am now an official "jailbird."

What surprised me most was that here deep in the "Bible Belt" is the 250-year-old Old Nick Williams Distillery. Located within eighteen minutes of where I live is the oldest distillery in the country. Founded in 1768 by Joseph Williams, the distillery has been in operation almost continuously except during the prohibition days. The distillery is located on family property. Most of the grains used in the process of making whiskey are grown on the property. I've known about North Carolina vineyards and old taverns, even mountain stills, but never legal whiskey making. Makes me wonder who of the great founding fathers was drinking all that fine whiskey.

COVID

Friday, November 12, 2021, I had felt weak after getting dressed and eating breakfast. A resident stopped by to tell me that a lady on our floor had died during the night. Recognizing that I looked pale, she asked if I was all right. I told her "no." About this time, another resident came to the apartment and surveying the situation said she would take me to the ER which she did. I waited only a few minutes before being seen in the ER but a long time in the ER. After about five hours of this test and that test and many "sticks," I was told I had COVID. Because I had been vaccinated and had had the booster shot, I told the nurse that I thought there was a mistake and could I be retested. My statement did not please the staff. I was told that indeed I had COVID and was being admitted as soon as a room was ready. In the meantime, I was moved to an ER holding room. There I stayed for another hour before being carted off to a very small room on a pulmonary COVID floor. One might call it the "Hospital Jail." A chair fit between the bed and a window. The hospital eating table was about a foot from the end of the chair. There was no way to get out of the bed on that side. A portable potty chair sat on the other side of the bed. The IV pole was on the same side as the potty chair. It was tricky but possible to get out of the bed on that side. Under the bed was a "magic lady" who would scream "Don't put your feet on the floor" if I tried to get out of bed at night.

All kinds of hospital personnel would come and go. Some were dressed in plastic from head to toe; others were not. "Why" I never asked. One doctor told me I had COVID with 2% pneumonia, another told me I had bronchitis, not pneumonia. But the lungs didn't seem to be the problem. The COVID complication seemed to be my blood pressure. Day and night, a nurse would come in to take my blood pressure standing up, sitting down, and laying down. It was a completely different hospital experience from the one I had had in April with an unexpected heart attack.

Sunday night, about 8:30 the cute little efficient head nurse swished into the room and asked if I wanted my password. "Password for what?" I asked. She flipped around and said: "Your pastor. He is downstairs and wants to see you." "Well, yes, send him up" was my reply. Ministers are the only visitors allowed for COVID patients. In about twenty minutes, he arrived, dressed in plastic and looking like a man from Mars. He came into the room just far enough that I could see him. Knowing that Sundays are long, hard days for ministers, I asked him why he had come so late. I certainly didn't expect a Sunday night visit from the minister. I had meant it as a compliment that he had come but, from his response, I think I had not chosen my words very carefully.

There was little entertainment in the hospital room. The small TV was high up on the wall and too far for me to read any words. The day I was admitted, my daughter had brought a plastic bag with some writing materials, a Bible, devotional booklets and a bridge magazine. I read the bridge magazine from cover to cover twice. Can't say the same for the Bible. The windows looked out to another building which was under some reconstruction but nothing was happening at the time. To gain strength and for something to do, I used the portable potty chair as a walker and pushed it around the bed, to the door at the far side of the room and back. Around and around I'd go. My hospital gown was long and straight, tied only at the neck. It would flap in the back when I walked. Had I thought about it, I could have pretended to be Lady Gaga and flipped the back side of the gown to the front and a leg to the side. That would have been fun. The doctor came each night and had me walk, (He never saw me with the potty chair.) After ten days, he decided I could return to my apartment.

I was in self-isolation for another ten days after the hospital stay. Instead of being in prison, I was only in jail. A resident got my post office box key and brought my mail to the small table at my door, rang the doorbell and left. Another resident delivered my newspaper to my door. Another left a thermos of coffee at the door. I ordered what meals I needed. After the ten days of isolation, I was able to return to normal activities. A month later the energy and stamina began slowly returning. To add insult to injury, Christmas day I was exposed to the new variant of COVID. Although not required, I did some self-isolation for a few days.

The N95 Mask

Two weeks ago I received an e-mail from PENTA (Piedmont Nose Ear and Throat) saying that all patients were required to wear a N95 mask when in the office. I was surprised that a particular type mask was being required. I called CVS to ask if they carried the N95 mask. They did not. So I called PENTA and asked where I could buy such a mask. The answer was Lowe's or Home Depot. Several days later I went to Home Depot and inquired about such a mask. The clerk replied that masks were on Aisle 7. I was surprised at the large selection of masks. Then I realized that construction workers need to wear a mask depending on the type work they do. The smallest package of N95 masks was $12.95 for eight masks.

At home, I opened the box and read the directions for how to place the mask on the face. It sounded a little complicated so I put the box away until closer to my appointment day. The night before my appointment, I got serious about putting on the mask. It was a real problem. The top strap went over the head and then the lower strap went over the head. The straps weren't long enough to go over my head, particularly with glasses on. I took the glasses off which helped some. Finally I got the thing on but realized it was probably on upside down. When I took it off, it pulled my wig off with it. This would never do at the doctor's office. I could put the mask on at home but would have to take it off at the office as my problem was in my nose. I had pictures of being in the office and the wig and mask flying off.

I made a plan. I would wear my usual good mask to the office. If questioned, I would explain that I had a N95 in my pocketbook but did not know how to put it on. Someone would have to help me put it on. When I got to the office, nothing was said about my not wearing a N95. Later I said something to the nurse about getting the e-mail and she told me that the mask I was wearing was fine. If it hadn't been they would have given me one.

I now have a box of eight N95 masks which I do not intend to wear unless Happy Home requires a mask at all times. Even then, I might just have to eat in my apartment as I am not going to have my wig fly off at the dinner table and land in someone's soup.

Birthday Adventure

It was early on a Saturday morning when my daughter Lisa and her husband picked me up for an adventure in the small community of Liberty, not far from Winston-Salem but in a rural area of the Piedmont region of North Carolina. Looking out the car window I wondered how these people voted and I began to realize that the basic needs of small communities are the same as larger ones. The mechanics of meeting the needs of two different lifestyles less than an hour apart must be difficult.

Rising Meadow Farm is a sheep raising farm and February 19, 2022, was Shearing Day in addition to being my birthday. Not everybody gets invited to Sheep Shearing Day to celebrate an 86th birthday.

The day was cold - colder and windier than I had anticipated when I dressed for this adventure. The parking lot was a "hike" from the farm buildings. Cars were parked along the sides of the dirt and gravel narrow road. When we got close to the buildings, Lisa stopped the car and told David to get out and change places with her. She wanted to pull over and park, but was too short to see where the side of the grass stopped and a deep drop-off began. From my seat, I could see and started "sending up prayers." David had no problem parking within two feet of the edge.

At the shearing shed we were told it would be twenty minutes before the next group of sheep would be brought up from the barn. People were leaving from the earlier shearing, so we were able to work our way up to the front of the enclosure. I was at a corner and could lean against a metal post. Some people had come from Charlotte others, from Raleigh and who knows where else. Little children would find their way to the front and stand around my legs. While waiting, I talked to the shearer who was born and raised on his family's sheep farm in Ireland. He now lives in Connecticut and does sheep shearing in the spring on the weekends. He told us that, after being sheared, sheep often fight among themselves as they do not recognize members of their flock. The hand-held shears which he uses are similar to those used for hundreds of years. He let me hold the shears. My hands were neither large enough nor strong enough to make them work. The shearer uses his legs and feet mostly to manage the animal. He wears special shoes that are softer than normal. Once a sheep has been sheared, it does not object to being sheared again.

When the next group of sheep approached the shed, they didn't want to come in. A "shepherd" pushed a little and convinced them to come. It was their first time to be sheared. In the group of five was one black sheep who was sheared first. The shearing process was fascinating. It started at the foot and went up the leg to the body. The wool was cut in long pieces. The cut wool from around the body was about six inches thick and at least twelve inches wide. The facial wool was clipped. When finished, the sheared wool was placed in a plastic bag, tagged, and taken from the shed to be sold. Many people had come to buy wool for their own use. The wool not sold during the shearing weekend is discarded.

My birthday adventure was an educational experience. I learned about sheep and realized how vulnerable they are and how easily they are led. It made me rethink some of the Biblical stories. It also caused me to wonder why "the black sheep" is used as a negative expression. In addition, my appreciation for people who work outside in cold weather increased greatly. (My feet thawed enough to bend only after arriving back home.)

Feelings

Asking someone "How are you?" is a common greeting that may or may not begin a conversation. Typically the reply is short. My usual reply is "Fine, thank you. How are you?" Depending on the situation, the conversation may or may not continue. At this point in time, I would like to express my true feelings which have been bubbling up in my entire being.

I'm tired of the 2020s. The 1920s roared but the 2020s can only yelp.

I'm tired of wearing a face mask.

I'm tired of my hearing aids getting caught in the straps of a mask.

I'm tired of a mask making it hard for me to breathe.

I'm tired of my glasses fogging up when wearing a mask in the cold.

I'm tired of my nose running under a mask.

I'm tired that my amusement of the day is trying to see how many gnats I can catch in a cup of vinegar.

I'm tired of the news on TV being consumed with COVID.

I'm tired of hearing about the January riots at the Capitol building.

I'm tired of hearing about Trump and all his shenanigans.

I'm tired of a racial "spin" put on any news event: be it a fire, a murder, or what have you. If it's not a racial "spin," it's a political "spin."

I'm tired of not feeling free to visit with friends because I might take COVID with me or bring it home.

I'm tired of having to recognize people by their shape or the way they walk or their hair or lack there of.

I'm tired of not feeling comfortable being with friends in a social setting without a mask.

I'm tired of being afraid to hug family members.

I'm tired of being afraid to go to events.

I'm tired of feeling like I am living in a cocoon.

Six months ago, things seemed to be looking up about COVID and life began bit by bit to return somewhat to normal. Then COVID came roaring back. According to the news, COVID is spreading less, but a new variant is emerging. Am I depressed? Yes. Am I going to take an antidepressant? No. I will continue to walk and talk with God about the situation. Hopefully, in a few more months we will be dancing in the streets.

Elevators

Recently I was on the second floor of the 400 Building waiting for the elevator. Earlier, while walking laps in the 500 Building I had "felt the need" to return quickly to my apartment. Consequently, I took a short cut to my building but I had to wait longer than usual for the elevator to arrive. When it finally arrived, two residents got off. However, a third man dressed in what appeared to be a Boy Scout uniform, remained on and asked where I was going. He also was going up but said I couldn't ride with him. In the meantime, two other men had appeared. One was wearing a shirt with Spectrum on the sleeve; the other was wearing a lanyard with his picture on it. I assumed that someone had a TV problem. The man on the elevator started talking to the other men. I realized that the man on the elevator was not a scout leader but an elevator repairman. He asked the man wearing the lanyard to ride with him. After the elevator door closed, I could hear men talking. It sounded as though they were talking in a tunnel. Eventually they returned. This time, when the elevator door opened, the repairman appeared to be standing on the top of the elevator with a large piece of equipment in front of him. I started to get on but the Spectrum man put his arm out to stop me and said that the elevator would be back. I wondered what I would hold onto when I was allowed on the elevator but, at this point in time, all I could worry about was

117

getting back to my apartment. When the elevator returned, there was no equipment, just the regular inside of the elevator. Questions remain: Was the man riding on some kind of platform? Was equipment on the elevator? Were my eyes playing tricks on me?

Yesterday, when I got on the elevator, the door closed with a loud click and, clear as a bell, it started talking to me. "What are you doing?" At first I was scared. Then I thought someone was probably standing outside the second floor door talking on a cell phone. Then, from within, came the reply, "Nothing." A talking elevator! By the time the elevator reached the first floor I noticed a red light close to the telephone sign on the wall. From where did the voices come? They knew each other. It was too early in the day for ghosts. Little old ladies should not have to deal with talking elevators.

If a talking elevator is not enough, today I stepped into a different elevator and its phone started ringing. Before I could answer it, the door closed and the ringing stopped.

This and That

"This and That" is a collection of a few of my recent experiences I thought interesting.

Several weeks ago, my bridge partner invited me to play bridge in the weekly bridge game at the Jewish Temple. It is a small group – only two tables. The folks were gracious and I was delighted to play. The group plays in the fellowship hall which is an extension of the sanctuary. The folding doors dividing the sanctuary and fellowship hall were open. I could see the stained-glass windows from the bridge table. I felt a little uncomfortable to be playing bridge in "The Lord's House." The next week the doors were closed and I felt completely at ease.

My son and his family have some type of group message app where they can "talk" back and forth and all can see and take part in the conversation. I am included but don't talk. I just look and read. My four-year old great-granddaughter often will watch, listen and make comments to her mother. She saw a picture of her year-old cousin and noticed the cousin had CROCS just like hers. Not knowing what CROCS were and thinking they were a type of toy, I later asked my daughter-in-law. They are a type of shoes. I've seen some CROCS at Happy Home and now wonder if originally CROCS were made for adults or for toddlers.

Speaking of shoes reminds me of socks. I was sitting at dinner with a new couple to Happy Home. They are excellent dancers and enjoy dancing anytime, anyplace music is played. This particular night we had music at dinner. My friend started talking about dancing and how dancing is done on the balls of the feet. As he was talking, he pulled out a package of white cloth bands which he proceeded to put on over his shoes. He had on shoes similar to tennis shoes. He placed the bands so they covered the shoes only in the area of the balls of his feet. I thought that was rather clever. His wife also pulled out her dancing socks and put them on over her shoes. When the next song started, they were off dancing.

A few days later I saw them dancing at supper but without dancing socks. Nothing would do except I had to get up and leave the table where I was sitting to ask about the dancing socks. Dan proudly pulled up his foot and showed me his plaid socks. Seems he was wearing leather sole shoes and didn't need dancing socks. I wondered if dancing socks were sold so, the next time I saw Dan, I asked him. Yes, just Google dancing socks and find out all about them.

For St. Patrick's Day, Happy Home had an Irish coffee party. We had a variety of many extra flavorings to add to our coffee. The hot coffee was delicious with special creamers and no "spirits." Chocolate spoons were provided to stir the hot coffee. Having never seen a two-toned chocolate spoon before, I was careful to stir a little, then eat a bit of the melting spoon, stir, drink a sip, stir, eat, drink etc. until the spoon was gone. I drank two cups of coffee and ate two spoons. Never thought I'd eat a spoon!

What different has happened to you today?

Made in the USA
Columbia, SC
20 December 2022

74635455R00072